# New Leadership of Civil Society Organisations

This book investigates the political, social, and economic dynamics and structures that influence the leadership of Civil Society Organisations at the local, national, and global levels.

Civil Society Organisations (CSOs) play an increasingly important role in the political, economic, and social dynamics that shape daily lives across the world. Encompassing a diverse range of organisations, objectives, and activities, the CSO sector is an expansive terrain characterised by dynamic relationships between leaders, agents of action, the communities, and the global challenges that drive their agenda, which span from poverty to climate emergency to injustice to inequalities. Drawing on case studies from Brazil, India, Yemen, Syria, Iran, and Turkey, this book explores the distinct challenges faced by CSO leaders, their current operational practices, and their strategies for future development. The book highlights the roles, contributions, and challenges of young CSO leaders in particular, at a time when they are taking an increasingly active role as agents for change and development.

Overall, the book emphasises the ways in which CSO leaders are not only shaped by profound challenges such as Covid-19, but also proactively react and respond. It will be of interest to researchers across the fields of global development, business studies, peacebuilding, international relations, and civil society.

**Ibrahim Natil** has published many works, including six books, taught at different academic institutions and worked for many civil society and international organisations. He is a Research Fellow at the Institute of International Conflict Resolution and Re-construction (IICRR) at Dublin City University, the Co-convenor of NGOs in Development Study Group, DSA-UK and the founder of Society Voice Foundation.

# Routledge Explorations in Development Studies

This Development Studies series features innovative and original research at the regional and global scale. It promotes interdisciplinary scholarly works drawing on a wide spectrum of subject areas, in particular politics, health, economics, rural and urban studies, sociology, environment, anthropology, and conflict studies.

Topics of particular interest are globalisation; emerging powers; children and youth; cities; education; media and communication; technology development; and climate change.

In terms of theory and method, rather than basing itself on any orthodoxy, the series draws broadly on the tool kit of the social sciences in general, emphasising comparison, the analysis of the structure and processes, and the application of qualitative and quantitative methods.

**Structural Transformation and Sustainable Development in the Global South**
An Integrated Approach
*Seung Jin Baek*

**Caribbean Regional Integration**
A Critical Development Approach
*Patsy Lewis*

**Leadership and Organisational Culture in Development**
Challenging Exceptionalism
*Violeta Schubert*

**New Leadership of Civil Society Organisations**
Community Development and Engagement
*Edited by Ibrahim Natil*

For more information about this series, please visit: www.routledge.com/Routledge-Explorations-in-Development-Studies/book-series/REDS

# New Leadership of Civil Society Organisations
Community Development and Engagement

**Edited by Ibrahim Natil**

LONDON AND NEW YORK

First published 2022
by Routledge
4 Park Square, Milton Park, Abingdon, Oxon OX14 4RN

and by Routledge
605 Third Avenue, New York, NY 10158

*Routledge is an imprint of the Taylor & Francis Group, an informa business*

© 2022 selection and editorial matter, Ibrahim Natil; individual chapters, the contributors

The right of Ibrahim Natil to be identified as the author of the editorial material, and of the authors for their individual chapters, has been asserted in accordance with sections 77 and 78 of the Copyright, Designs and Patents Act 1988.

All rights reserved. No part of this book may be reprinted or reproduced or utilised in any form or by any electronic, mechanical, or other means, now known or hereafter invented, including photocopying and recording, or in any information storage or retrieval system, without permission in writing from the publishers.

*Trademark notice*: Product or corporate names may be trademarks or registered trademarks, and are used only for identification and explanation without intent to infringe.

*British Library Cataloguing-in-Publication Data*
A catalogue record for this book is available from the British Library

*Library of Congress Cataloging-in-Publication Data*
A catalog record has been requested for this book

ISBN: 978-1-032-26398-4 (hbk)
ISBN: 978-1-032-26399-1 (pbk)
ISBN: 978-1-003-28814-5 (ebk)

DOI: 10.4324/9781003288145

Typeset in Times new roman
by Deanta Global Publishing Services, Chennai, India

# Contents

*Contributors*   vii

1. **Introducing New Leaders of Civil Society Organisations**   1
   IBRAHIM NATIL

2. **Exploring New Concepts and Practices of Civil Society Organisations' Leadership**   8
   IBRAHIM NATIL

3. **Four-pillars Approach to Effective Management and Leadership: Humanitarian Aid and Development Assistance CSOs**   16
   MAHMOUD ALMADHOUN

4. **CSOs Leaders between Covid-19 and Technology Platforms: Peacebuilding Case Study**   28
   BASSAM KASSOUMEH

5. **Common Minimum Universe: Role of Youth Leadership in Community Development**   41
   VIJAYENDRA KADALABAL, SWATHI POTTABATHINI, KUMAR GAURAV

6. **Women's Movements in Turkey: Patriarchal Authoritarianism from Empire to Republic**   55
   FRESIA SABETI AND MOHSEN MOHEIMANY

7. **The Tale of Reformism in Iran**   68
   NADER GANJI

## Contents

8  **The Formation of a Municipal 'Third Sector' in Brazil**  80
   CÍCERO AUGUSTO SILVEIRA BRAGA, MUCIO TOSTA GONÇALVES,
   THIAGO PERIARD

9  **Constant Swings: Women's Rights Movements in the Era of Islamic Republic of Iran**  98
   MOHSEN MOHEIMANY AND MAHDIEH GOLROO

10 **Effective Leadership: Yemeni Local CSOs**  110
   ELHAM RAWEH

11 **Conclusion: Impact and Ways Forward**  121
   IBRAHIM NATIL

   *Index*  127

# Contributors

**Mahmoud Almadhoun** is a winner of the German Academic Exchange Services (DAAD) award. He earned his PhD in business from Regensburg University-Germany (2010). In his studies, he concentrated on value chain analysis and competitive advantage of the small and medium-sized enterprises (SMEs) and on total quality management (TQM) impact on industrial firms' competitiveness. Prior to joining the Community College of Qatar in 2019, Dr. Almadhoun had a substantial business and management tutoring background. Dr. Almadhoun is an Adair Action-Centred Leadership (ACL) accredited trainer (John Adair's Leadership Framework). He is also a CHS Alliance approved trainer on Core Humanitarian Standard.

**Thiago Periard do Amaral** holds a BA in economics from University of Juiz de Fora (2004), MSc in Industrial Economics from University of Santa Catarina (2007) and PhD in Economics from Fluminense University (2013). He was a substitute professor in the Department of Economics and Finance at UFJF (2006–2008) and a project analyst at the Development Bank of the Extreme South (2008). He worked for eight years as a Full Economist at Petrobras (2008–2015), at Petrobras University, where he dedicated himself to the company's Energy Economics courses. Currently, he is a Professor at the Federal University of São João del-Rei.

**Cícero Augusto Silveira Braga** holds a BA in economics from University of São João del Rei (2016) and a MSc (2018) and PhD (2021) in applied economics from University of Viçosa. Cicero's main research focus lies on microeconometric and development analysis. He is currently working at the World Bank at the Poverty and Equity Global Practice.

**Nader Ganji** is a PhD graduate of University of Tehran in public policy. He also holds an MA with distinction from the University of

Nottingham and a BA from the University of Tehran. Being a university lecturer and researcher in Iran, he specialises in organised religion, history, political structures, class conflict, and institutional and group theories.

**Kumar Gaurav** is a Senior Executive at SABAL, Tata Steel Rural Development Society (TATA Steel CSR) and is an expert in the development paradigm of disability and for the past five years has worked in tribal-dominated states of Jharkhand and Odisha. He also uses cinema as a medium to promote awareness among indigenous communities. As a student he was engaged in several social advocacy initiatives through theatre art, which he continues to pursue. During the Covid-19 pandemic he worked extensively on ground-level relief and awareness initiatives among the marginalised communities.

**Mahdieh Golroo** holds an MA in economic development, is a veteran activist of the Iranian student movement with an interest in women's rights. As a researcher of women's rights and a commentator of Iranian politics, Mahdieh is an affiliate of the PEN Institute in Sweden and published pieces of reports about women movements.

**Mucio Tosta Gonçalves** is Professor at Universidade Federal de São João del Rei (UFSJ), in Minas Gerais, Brazil. PhD in development, agriculture and society at Universidade Federal Rural do Rio de Janeiro. Professor at the Postgraduate Program in Territorial Development and Planning – PGDPLAT/UFSJ between 2019 and 2021. Mucio has experience in economics and sociology, focusing on political economy; history of economic thought; collective strategies; and forest plantations economy and policy. This chapter received financial support from the 'Research Fund' from the Dean for Research and Postgraduate Programs (PROPE) of UFSJ, whom we thank.

**Vijayendra Kadalabal** is a development professional who currently leads a youth movement called Yuva Shakti which nurtures 5,000+ grassroots youth to become constitutionally aware and human rights defenders. He has over seven years' experience in working with Children and Youth across India including some of the remotest States of Chhattisgarh, Jharkhand, and Odisha. He is a Chevening Scholar and has a master's degree in financial economics, social work, and international development. An inherent believer in the 'power of collective,' he is also a hodophile, a passionate trekker, a movie buff, and a trained Classical Carnatic singer.

**Bassam Kassoumeh** is an international researcher focusing on peacebuilding, conflict resolution and transformation, governance, and state-building. He's been working in the humanitarian and development sector since 2014. Having lived through conflict, he has decided to work in peacebuilding, and conflict resolution and transformation. He has also worked for ACLED, as a Syria researcher, and published two analysis pieces. He also published a journal article on the effects of Covid-19 on peacebuilding, focusing on the contexts of Yemen, Syria, and the South Caucasus. He is currently the lead researcher exploring the uses of blockchain technology and cryptocurrencies in peacebuilding.

**Mohsen Moheimany** holds a PhD in political science, and he is a journalist and researcher with an interest in Iran's politics and civil society. Mohsen has written two book chapters on the contemporary trajectory of Iranian civil society, its latest developments, and also a book about the political opportunities and constraints of NGOs in hybrid regimes.

**Ibrahim Natil** is a Research fellow at Institute of International Conflict Resolution and Re-construction (IICRR) at DCU and the Co-convenor of NGOs in Development Study Group at DSA-UK. He is a Professor (Ass) of International Relations at Joaan Bin Jassim Academy for Defence Studies. He has been invited as a guest and visiting lecturer to a number of universities and has acted as an external examiner at Glasgow Caledonian University (2021), Durham University (2020), and Bradford University (2018/2021). He is the winner of Robert Chamber Best Overall Paper, selected by DSA Ireland (2017) and edited/authored many works, including *Conflict, Civil Society, and Women's Empowerment* (2021) and *Hamas Transformation Opportunities and Challenges* (2015). He is the book editor of *Youth Civic Engagement in the Middle East and North Africa* (Routledge, 2021), and the leading editor of *Barriers to Effective Civil Society Organisations: Political, Social and Funding Shifts* (Routledge, 2020) and *Power of Civil Society in the Middle East and North Africa: Peacebuilding, Change and Development* (Routledge, 2019). He also writes for *Independent Australia*. He also authored and published several articles and book chapters on a wide range of international relations, politics, and development including civil society, conflict resolution, and human security. He worked for many CSOs and international NGOs, was the founding director of the Society Voice Foundation (2002–2010), and managed more than 60 community projects in the field of human rights, community peacebuilding, and women and youth empowerment since 1997.

**Swathi Pottabathini** is a policy enthusiast who currently works as a Senior Project Associate at the Centre for Effective Governance of Indian States (CEGIS). She is extremely passionate about creating impact at the grassroots through evidence-based policy interventions and Gandhi's talisman has been her constant source of inspiration. She worked at a grassroots NGO with tribals, before taking up the role of a Chief Program Officer at GramHeet to work with smallholder farmers. She is a Caux Scholar-Asia Plateau and Lead Like a Girl Fellow. She loves to create sustainable art, practice yoga, read voraciously, write wholeheartedly, and travel extensively.

**Elham Raweh** is a project manager at Saferworld, a leading NGO working in preventing violent conflict. She worked with several NGOs as a consultant, manager, coordinator, trainer, and facilitator. She holds an MA in conflict management and humanitarian assistance. She is an activist, researcher, and consultant in Yemeni affairs.

**Fresia Sabeti** has a BA in journalism, and is a women's rights activist and journalist in Turkey. With two decades of experience in political and women's rights activism, currently she works in the field of Turkish politics and society. Fresia wrote several reports about the situation of women in Iran and Turkey.

# 1 Introducing New Leaders of Civil Society Organisations

*Ibrahim Natil*

## Introduction

The Covid-19 pandemic has imposed complicated challenges on all economic, educational, social services, and development sectors. The pandemic has not distinguished between rich and poor, local, national and international, or small, medium, and large organisations. It also imposes barriers to leadership, civic space, and civil society engagement at large. Civic space is given to civil society organisations (CSOs); however, this has been shrinking owing to the emerging and complicated environments of financial uncertainty, social restrictions, and political barriers. These uncertainties have motivated and pushed the majority of CSOs' leaders to think outside the box and act differently to keep their work, operations, interventions, and deliveries going in different locations, cultures, and communities around the world. However, the pandemic today is amongst other challenges facing our world owing to the lack of 'effective leadership,' as Bennis defines it (2007). This book discusses the existing literature to explore and compare the definitions of CSOs' local leadership structures in different case studies and countries. This follows the work of long-term scholars in the field like Vroom and Jago, who define leadership as a 'process of motivating people to work together collaboratively to accomplish great things' (2007: 18). The concept of effective leadership and competent organisation to face the threats and challenges of the modern world are more important now than ever before (Bisbee, 2007; Zaccaro, 2007).

This book presents a theoretical and empirical contribution developed around the following questions: How does CSOs' leadership differ from leadership in other sectors? What are its distinctive dimensions, if any? Which innovative/alternative forms might CSOs' leadership take? What strategies, processes and material conditions encourage leadership development in CSOs? What are the distinctive challenges faced by CSOs' leaders? To what extent and how does CSO leadership promote equality and justice

DOI: 10.4324/9781003288145-1

within the CSO sector in the circumstances of the global pandemic? What are the dark sides of CSO leadership, and what can be learnt from them? The book provides up-to-date case studies analysis on CSOs' leadership and barriers to engagement, challenges to development opportunities, and lessons learnt on changes in India, Yemen, Brazil, Turkey, Syria, and Iran. It is innovative and different as it mainly stems from the experiences and fieldwork of young contributors from these regions, enriching the debate on various developments with new insights and a fresh perspective, particularly from the Global South. This focuses on challenges facing CSOs' leadership's societal contributions, current operational practices, and strategies for future development. CSOs are playing an increasingly important role in shaping our daily lives across the world despite the fact of shifts in political, financial, social, and health dynamics, as Natil (2020) discusses.

A CSO is an independent actor that assists 'people to claim their rights in promoting rights-based approaches, in shaping development policies and partnerships and in overseeing their implementation' (Busan Global Partnership Forum for Effective Development Cooperation, 2011; see also UNDP, 2013: 123; OECD, 2011: 10). CSOs are created by a group of volunteers representing civil society to play a powerful role in raising awareness of citizens' active participation, as well as defending their rights in all aspects of life. CSOs include a diverse set of organisations, ranging from small, informal, community-based organisations to the large international non-governmental organisations (INGOs) working through local CSOs across countries of the Global South (UNDP, 2013: 123). However, organisations such as trade unions or professional associations, not-for-profit universities, and research institutes also define themselves as CSOs. The Development Assistance Committee (DAC) of the Organisation for Economic Co-operation and Development (OECD) defines CSOs as follows:

> can be defined to include all non-market and non-state organizations outside of the family in which people organize themselves to pursue shared interests in the public domain. Examples include community-based organizations and village associations, environmental groups, women's rights groups, farmers' associations, faith-based organizations, labour unions, co-operatives, professional associations, chambers of commerce, independent research institutes and the not-for-profit media.
>
> (OECD, 2011: 10)

The book provides overviews of some international donors' interests and values in supporting strong leadership for CSOs. It also discusses some international donors' interests and values in supporting CSOs' projects during the Covid-19 pandemic. Some chapters examine the impact of well-educated and experienced CSO leadership structures on local politics, power and its impact on social and political life. This includes introducing the lessons gained from certain CSO leaders despite political restrictions, absence of freedoms, divisions, conflict, social conservatism, and lack of opportunities. In addition, chapters' contributors analyse the extent to which CSOs' new and young leadership teams have employed social media and various technology platforms to facilitate the operations of their organisations during the Covid-19 pandemic. This shows the power of young leadership teams to contribute to making change a reality in terms of peace, security, and development (Pruitt & Lee-Koo, 2020).

The contributors are young scholars whose in-depth community experiences are supported by intensive fieldwork, participatory observation, literature reviews, and strong arguments. They also aim to explore how CSOs' leaders are currently engaging in various contexts, which is important for different target groups, including scientists, researchers, national-level policymakers, donors, CSOs' staff, and the beneficiaries themselves. Each of these groups has different communications needs. These processes often undermine and block CSOs' scope of work, engagement, and contribution to development and change processes. In many contexts, however, it is largely about the ways CSOs' leaders engage in civil society actions and programmes. This will be an influential work as it contains in-depth understanding and evidence of particular CSOs' leaders' engagement in development, human rights, politics, social change, and community peacebuilding actions. Presenting up-to-date empirical research helps to understand the significance of the engagement and contribution of CSOs' leaders to grassroots actions in the fields of development, peacebuilding, and civic engagement.

The book also tackles the impact of Covid-19 on CSOs' leadership in terms of their operations, effectiveness, and efficiency of their contribution to change and community development processes. It discusses a number of definitions in reference to local culture, social background, and political contexts. The chapters are structured around the theme of the CSOs' leadership in development actions and practice, and they are further subdivided into 'engaging leadership' and 'adapting leadership' to ensure the efficiency and effectiveness of CSOs' leadership in terms of their development and engagement. The book is divided into 11 chapters, which are grouped by the overall theme: the new leadership of CSOs. Ibrahim Natil's chapters include the background, framework, scope, questions of study, and methods and provide sound theoretical and structural context for the reader in which to place each individual case study and chapter. The introduction and conclusion also place the scope of the book into the wider framework of the academic discussion about the topic, so there are clear references to related materials and the themes within which this book is situated. The other chapters are empirical, but each one also discusses the theories and methodologies relevant to its country case study. Therefore, a balance between theoretical/methodological and empirical discussions is ensured.

All material in this book consists of research to provide an exceptional book based on the academic and professional experiences of the editor and young scholars in the field of civil society leadership. For example, leadership mechanisms, capabilities, and tools are of great importance for the efficiency and effectiveness of CSOs' programmes and actions, as Mahmoud Almadhoun discusses in Chapter 3 by introducing a five-dimension approach for the effective management and leadership of humanitarian aid and development assistance CSOs. This approach also assists with understanding new concepts and practices by CSO leaders who have shifted their leadership mechanism owing to Covid-19 barriers, and as Bassam Kassoumeh introduces a peacebuilding case study in Chapter 4 to discuss the role of CSO leaders in employing technology platforms during the Covid-19 pandemic.

Young CSO leaders are considered significant agents for change and development in their societies in responding to shifts due to Covid-19. They have a considerable impact and influence on social and political life in the fields of human rights and peacebuilding. This volume was keen to publish research that provides up-to-date analysis on the challenges and constraints facing young new leaders of CSOs in the fields of development, change, and political challenges. Cho et al. (2020) have previously discussed digital civic engagement by young civil society leaders. However, young leaders have been very resilient to the current circumstances of the pandemic. UNICEF's Jordan representative, Tanya Chapuisat, said:

> I am inspired by the resilience and the leadership shown by the youth volunteers who refused to let this pandemic break their spirit, instead they volunteered online to share lifesaving information, packed food parcels and took care of the most vulnerable in their community.
> (UNICEF, 2020)

The pandemic, which has forced CSO leaders to move peacebuilding dialogue to online and virtual spaces, offered new opportunities for the inclusion of typically marginalised and conflict-affected groups in peacebuilding activities. Digital platforms are vehicles that can improve the participation of minorities and those typically marginalised, such as women and youth. Further, digital platforms are expected to contribute to conducive peace since the inclusion of those affected by conflict in peacebuilding dialogue results in long-lasting reconciliation. These young contributors are from different nations (Brazil, India, Yemen, Syria, Iran, and Turkey) to promote cooperation between societies and communities across the world so as to advance our understanding of how CSO leadership can contribute to making societies more just and equal. Francesca Polletta (2016) has previously discussed the participatory enthusiasm and significance for engagement, where CSO leaders can practise their skills and knowledge freely to change lives in their societies.

Covid-19 has pushed the localisation agenda and enforced systems to change, giving more power and autonomy to local CSO leaders, as INGOs are no longer on the ground due to travel restrictions imposed by the pandemic. This hybrid leadership is self-reflective in nature and relies on effective leader-follower collaboration, which is conducive to sustainable peace. Engaging and effective leadership is a condition to achieve sustainable peace in the current health crisis. In Chapter 5, Kumar Gaurav, Swathi Pottabathini, and Vijayendra Kadalabal investigate what the role of the local leadership of CSOs is in combating the pandemic in India. India faced a unique challenge with the public health crisis, which is now turning into what was an avoidable humanitarian crisis. This is the result of the direct political, social, and economic impact of the 'lockdown' imposed by the state to deal with the pandemic. Marginalised groups, such as women, are still paying a high price. However, their engagement and raising of their voices show a distinguished style of leadership in these marginalised communities, Serena Cosgrove (2010) argues.

Women's rights issues have been controversial and challenging for civil society leadership in certain restrictive political contexts. Women's rights movements, after more than a century of fighting for social and political rights, have faced an uplift in patriarchal authoritarianism in the 21st century, as Mohsen Moheimany, Fresia Sabeti and Mahdieh Golroo discuss in Chapter 6. The authors discuss cases of women who were inspired by global waves of feminism, and, through limited state-run reforms, hundreds of feminist groups and activists succeeded in gradually appealing for certain rights in areas such as family laws and political participation. However, in the period 2000–2020, the states of Iran and Turkey steered back towards an updated version of patriarchal authoritarianism by resorting to law manipulation, security measures, and political engineering. This pushed back the growing women's rights movements and downgraded their demands to basic rights. Moheimany, Sabeti, and Golroo discuss the trajectory of the two states in confrontation with women's rights movements in the 21st century and show how CSOs' leaders have employed radical Islamic discourse and a stringent set of policies to contain feminist movements.

Women's civil rights and a pluralist civil society, however, are challenged by the supposed process of reforms. In Chapter 7, Nader Ganji discusses the tale of reformism in Iran and why reformers have constantly failed to achieve real change in terms of civil society, which has had a serious impact on leadership in this sector as well. Ganji analyses four main historical eras: from constitutional reformism to the coup (1905–1921), from suffocation to resurgence (1925–1953), from coup to revolution (1953–1979), and from revolution to revolutionary reformism (1979–1997). Prevailing narratives attribute the emergence and growth of the Iranian reformists to their interaction with their European counterparts. The author studies the impact of CSOs' leadership on the reforming process as well.

CSOs' or 'third sector' formation in Brazil is discussed in Chapter 8, where Cícero Augusto Silveira Braga, Mucio Tosta Gonçalves, and Thiago Periard review the literature and report some interviews they conducted to explain what the third sector is and what its roles are in capitalist society in Brazil. They also analyse some theoretical elements concerning actors' conformation in the so-called third sector and discuss the experience of a non-governmental organisation that was created and has been operating for more than 18 years in an industrial municipality in the state of Minas Gerais, Brazil.

The impact of effective local leadership from CSOs is a pivotal issue and has been a controversial debate in the field of civil society and the non-profit sector owing to a number of shifts in the political landscape, donors' agenda and priorities, and social dynamics and contexts (Natil, 2020, 2021). Elham Raweh discusses local leadership in Chapter 9 by presenting a case study of Yemeni CSOs' sustainability. Raweh collected primary data from direct and personal interviews with CSOs' leaders to assess their leadership quality in contributing to Yemeni civil society. Yemeni civil society has evolved over the years, forming different shapes for different purposes. It was documented that the early forms that existed in the 1950s were against the colonial rule in the south and against the Imamate in the north. Civil society evolved further over the years until the 1990s after the unification of southern and northern Yemen, when the new constitution guaranteed the right to form groups in different shapes and for different activities (political, social, and voluntary). Many CSOs were established and developed civil society engagement, but after the escalation of the conflict in 2015, many CSOs had to change their activities or, in the worst cases, shut down.

Finally, the volume presents a number of remarks, recommendations, and lessons. In Chapter 11, Ibrahim Natil delivers a concise conclusion by drawing implications and indicating future directions. He also explores the effects of marginalisation on civil society and proposes recommendations to CSOs' leaders to minimise these effects. The book's chapters also examine these experiences and cases studies of leaders' engagement in their CSOs' activities. CSO leaders' contributions to active public engagement – based on peacebuilding, development, human rights, politics, and change processes at different levels – are varied and contextual.

## References

Bennis, W. (2007). The challenge of leadership in the modern world: Introduction to special issue. *American Psychologist, 62*, 2–5.

Bisbee, D. C. (2007). Looking for leaders: Current practices in leadership identification in higher education. *Planning and Changing, 38*, 77–88.

Busan Global Partnership Forum for Effective Development Cooperation. (2011). Fourth High Level Forum on Aid Effectiveness. *Busan, Republic of Korea*, 29 November–1 December 2011. Accessed July 24, 2020. https://www.oecd.org/dac/effectiveness/49650173.pdf.

Cho, A., Byrne, J., & Pelter, Z. (2020). *Digital civic engagement by young people*. UNICEF Offices of Global Insight and Policy. Accessed January 5, 2021. https://www.unicef.org/sites/default/files/2020-07/Digital-civic-engagement-by-young-people-2020_4.pdf.

Cosgrove, S. (2010). *Leadership from the margins: Women and civil society organisations in Argentina*. Rutgers University Press.

Natil, I. (2020). Introducing barriers to effective civil society organisations. In I. Natil, V. Malila, & Y. Sai (Eds.), *Barriers to effective civil society organisations: Political, social and financial shifts*. Routledge.

Natil, I. (2021). *Youth civic engagement and local peacebuilding in the Middle East and North Africa: Prospects and challenges for community development*. Routledge.

OECD. (2011). *How DAC members work with civil society organisations: An overview*. Accessed February 27, 2020. https://www.oecd.org/dac/peer-reviews/Final_How_DAC_members_work_with_CSOs%20ENGLISH.pdf.

Polletta, F. (2016). Participatory enthusiasms: A recent history of citizen engagement initiatives. *Journal of Civil Society, 12*(3), 231–246. https://doi.org/10.1080/17448689.2016.1213505

Pruitt, L., & Lee-Koo, K. (2020). *Young women and leadership*. Routledge.

UNDP. (2013). *Working with civil society in foreign aid*. Accessed February 25, 2020. https://www.undp.org/content/dam/undp/documents/partners/civil_society/publications/2013_UNDP-CH-Working-With-Civil-Society-in-Foreign-Aid_EN.pdf.

UNICEF. (2020). *Youth led initiative fund launched on international volunteering day*. Accessed January 4, 2021. https://www.unicef.org/jordan/press-releases/youth-led-initiative-fund-launched-international-volunteering-day.

Vroom, V. H., & Jago, A. G. (2007). The role of the situation in leadership. *American Psychologist, 62*(1), 17–24.

Zaccaro, S. J. (2007). Trait-based perspectives of leadership. *American Psychologist, 62*(1), 6–16.

# 2 Exploring New Concepts and Practices of Civil Society Organisations' Leadership

*Ibrahim Natil*

## Introduction

CSOs' active leadership and engagement in grassroots activities can help to decide on changes to their society despite conflict, a lack of policies, a restrictive political environment, and the complexity of the sociocultural and economic contexts. It also discusses concepts of 'effective leadership' and 'participatory leadership engagement,' where active leaders have the power to decide on changes to their future. This volume seeks to present a number of case studies of 'adapting leadership' and 'effective leadership' in the field of the civil society/non-profit sector to discuss threats and challenges in responding to the Covid-19 pandemic. However, the threats facing the world today are owed to a lack of effective leadership from our human institutions, as Bennis (2007) discusses. Institutions, including CSOs, need competent leaders to solve these problems, owing to uncertainties and complexities. Çitaku et al. (2012) categorise leadership competencies into five domains: social responsibility, innovation, self-management, task management, and justice orientation. These categories are applicable to the CSOs' scope of work and essential components, elements in their missions, and their visions and goals, in addition to their capacity to adapt to shifts and challenges.

As integral parts of CSOs' scope of work, CSOs' leaders should be fully aware of these categories of leadership competence and themes of civil society, community development, and engagement. Local organisations are always challenged by a rapidly and significantly changing environment, which requires the leadership and managerial levels to respond to the demands of change, as Alan Fowler and Chiku Malunga (2020) argue. This provides more chances for CSOs' leaders to understand the turbulences facing local groups in the field of management and development, as David Lewis (2014) explains.

In short, this chapter raises and addresses the following questions: To what extent have new CSO leaders actually succeeded in achieving their

DOI: 10.4324/9781003288145-2

objectives despite shifts, technical constraints, and policy challenges? What is the role of CSO leaders in overcoming the challenges/restrictions/societal shifts facing their operations, deliveries, and intervention? How have new leaders of local and grassroots organisations overcome challenges in these societies? This volume focuses on themes of leadership in civil society, community development, and engagement actions by examining specific civil society case studies in India, Yemen, Brazil, Turkey, Syria, and Iran. It aims at improving our understanding of how these issues/themes are influencing the way CSOs' leaders contribute, deliver, intervene, and position themselves in various societies effectively and efficiently.

## Engaging Leadership

In principle, CSOs' leaders seek to promote grassroots civic engagement to make a real change in marginalised and/or vulnerable groups in a process called 'participatory democracy'. This process of civic engagement is also associated with the practice of a top-down mechanism conducted by engaging and effective leaders who contribute to the improvement of the public sector and development of civil society. The concepts of 'effective leadership' and 'participatory engagement' are discussed here where active leaders have the power to decide on changes to their future. The volume also discusses the significance of the relationship between CSOs' leadership structures and the civic grassroots level and its impact on community development, engagement, and change processes. However, the relationship between CSO leaders of mass-based organisations often compete over public space, legitimacy, and resources, as Islah Jad (2007, 2018) argues.

This discussion assists the reader to understand CSO leaders' skills, knowledge, capacities, contributions, and power by exploring the challenges facing them in reference to development and change. The authors build on and discuss their practical and academic experience by introducing a four-dimension approach to the effective management and leadership of humanitarian aid and development assistance CSOs as Almadhoun discusses in Chapter 3. This approach provides a comprehensive guide for those with management and leadership responsibilities in humanitarian CSOs and NGOs at large. It addresses strategy and organisational development, human resources, training and capacity building, partnership with stakeholders, resource mobilisation, and organisational excellence. Particular emphasis is placed upon the different challenges faced by leadership structures from different locations and cultures that are linked not only to conflict, social, cultural, and financial constraints but also to technical issues and policies that are crucial markers of development and change. These constraints have already imposed serious challenges to the effective leadership of CSOs and their scope of work and intervention in various fields, such as education, health, peacebuilding, human rights, improving livelihoods, unemployment, and infrastructure (Natil, 2021, 2020).

This assists in understanding other experiences and definitions of managing non-profit organisations or the third sector, emphasising effective leadership and governance, as Mike Hudson (2017) argues. However, social capital for the third sector is a very significant element in encouraging civil society leaders to promote trust among various civil society actors, victims, and/or marginalised groups in divided societies owing to conflict or cultural, political, or ideological differences. In this context, in Chapter 8, Cícero Augusto Silveira Braga, Mucio Tosta Gonçalves, and Thiago Periard discuss the oscillation of the management of this type between formality and informality, not least because it depends on the role(s) that the founders play in the construction of organisational identity and in obtaining financial and political support from public and private agents and the grassroots level. The authors discuss the elements of building the identity of a local actor in the third sector, pointing out that the form of intervention of the organisation studied in the municipal social space has made it visible and socially relevant, although it has distanced itself from the construction of alternatives for social transformation. As intermediaries between social forces and their demands and the state, third sector organisations assume complementary functions in the field of public policies and social action, although they can contribute to (and within) processes of resistance and social change in the context of capitalism.

CSO leaders' understanding of these technical constraints, financial shifts, and societal complexities is a prerequisite for the planning and implementation of change strategies and tactics based on development and rights agendas. For example, women's rights groups, their process of engagement, and their leadership are challenged owing to social, political, and financial shifts and the risks of Covid-19, as Natil (2021) discusses. To what extent have 'marginalised leaders' of women's rights movements contributed to a new structure of civil society? This complicated relationship between local leadership and civil society and its impact on grassroots participation in the processes of decision-making and the development of their society is discussed by Jad (2018). Serena Cosgrove (2010) argues that women who have lived on the margins of their communities have contributed to the improvement of their civil society by challenging the patriarchal systems of power after decades of economic and political repression. Repressive contexts challenged young women who lived on the margins of their society; however, they have struggled to lead a rights movement for change, as Mohsen Moheimany, Fresia Sabeti, and Mahdieh Golroo discuss in Chapters 6 and 9. They have contributed an exceptional case study by exploring the role of the women's civil society rights movements in Turkey and Iran.

This allows us to understand the complexity of the relationships between marginalised 'leaders' and grassroots women's movements, as well as the challenges facing women, which have already placed vulnerable groups in a worse situation, remaining on the margins of society, as discussed by Natil (2021). These complexities of the relationships among community leaders, victims, and marginalised groups assist leaders to explore how to lead their CSOs more effectively, as Mike Hudson (2017) discusses. Remarkably, although considerable research has highlighted the weaknesses and limitations of CSOs' leaders' influence and power, rather less attention has been paid to the legislation and policies that have resulted in the exceptional circumstances and dynamics characterising some societies in which CSOs' leaders find themselves. Some CSOs' leaders, for example, have campaigned to change political cultures and social dynamics due to their playing significant roles in and making contributions to national and local elections and politics. This will contribute to making a change to women's rights by endorsing and enacting, for example, quotas to increase women's rights and political representation in local councils and parliaments, as the Society Voice Foundation (SVF) and other local CSOs do in Palestine (Amer, 2021). Raising awareness of marginalised groups such as women, however, remains a serious challenge for CSOs' leaders in terms of how these groups will engage in change and development processes without real political participation in a conflict zone, as Natil (2021) discusses.

This is a part of distinct struggles that occur when different classes, political ideologies, and marginalisation contribute to shaping styles of leadership, tactics, and movements' strategies, as Serena Cosgrove (2010) argues. Therefore, this volume offers new insights into how CSOs' leaders in such countries are not only shaped by but also react to shifts, policies, conflicts, constraints, and challenges. Mike Hudson (2017) discusses how to manage CSOs and their relationships with marginalised groups with greater efficiency and govern them with enhanced energy in his fully revised guide to civil society management. This reflects Cosgrove's (2010) argument on how the power of CSOs' leaders has contributed to the direction of women's rights on local, regional, and global development agendas. The role of leadership is particularly significant when challenging these complexities within various groups. This assists the target groups in working together in compelling new mechanisms in which active CSO leaders initiate and formalise plans, programmes, activities, practices and the motivations of victims and target groups, as Laura Graham (2016) discusses.

Covid-19, for instance, has been a strong case study to indicate and prove that a CSO's leader has to have had experience, self-reliance, and the power to engage with local people, volunteers, and staff, as well as innovation to think outside the box. These are examples of leaders' capacity to adopt new strategies and policies to accommodate their programmes and activities when responding to landscape shifts within their societies, as Natil (2021) argues.

## Adapting Leadership

Bennis (2007) argues that the threat challenging the world today is because of the lack of effective leadership of our organisations. The leadership of CSOs or non-profit organisations around the world, for example, has recently faced serious challenges, owing to Covid-19 and threats to societies at large. There have been, however, leaders who failed to adapt their CSOs' plans, techniques, and deliveries to meet the demands and the needs of their target groups, volunteers, and staff, owing to the health shifts due to Covid-19. The leaders of these organisations must play an essential role in directing, motivating, and developing the capacities of staff and volunteers, as Estrada and Carranza (2016) discuss. Leaders should act in accordance with the local cultures, social dynamics, and economic demands and needs, as Natil (2021) discusses with regard to the role of local leaders and their CSOs in influencing the decision-making process to protect women from domestic violence.

Covid-19 has forced non-profit organisations or CSOs to balance their acts by adapting to new leadership strategies and governance structures, as Caitlin McMullin and Paloma Raggo (2020) argue. In other words, these leaders should think and behave locally, despite the fact that the pandemic has been a common global issue. Leaders' sense of direction is also reflected in the CSOs' direct and indirect beneficiaries and target groups through the implementation, monitoring, and evaluation of community activities, programmes, and projects. CSOs' leaders serve as agents for social change, development, and peacebuilding in responding to the demands and the needs of their beneficiaries and target groups at the local, national, and/or international levels where they operate and engage, as Natil (2021) argues.

Leaders' capacities in this context show their charismatic power for change, as Estrada and Carranza (2016) discuss. Transformational leaders are spontaneous and successful in making a real change in responding to crises or conflict situations by delivering security of measurements and/or actions to stablise the CSO itself, as Estrada and Carranza (2016) discuss. The concept of a transformational, collective, place-based, deliberative, pluralistic, and participatory leadership style to ensure equitable and meaningful participation and inclusion is discussed in Chapter 3. Such leaders are charismatic, admired by their followers and intellectuals, and look after their volunteers' and staff's needs. Leaders who rely on volunteers are considered transformational leaders when engaging with them in responding to crises. Leaders' behaviours and attitudes when managing a crisis are essential to show their mental power, flexibility, knowledge, and skills. In Chapter 5, Kumar Gaurav, Swathi Pottabathini, and Vijayendra Kadalabal investigate the role of the efficiency of a voluntary group of individuals and its leadership, who choose to collaborate using digital platforms and their personal networks and mobilise resources (financial and non-financial), and which has assisted more than 30,000 individuals to date with coping with hunger. Based on the analysis, the authors seek to understand how youth and their leadership in community development are enabling a connection that is both global and also assisting individuals to deal with local-level challenges to be part of what the authors call a 'common minimum universe.'

New CSO leaders should be digitally oriented and equipped with skills that they employ when engaging with various audiences and professionals from different backgrounds and cultures, such as local communities, academics, and international partners, including donors and diplomats. CSOs' leaders also engage in public diplomacy activities with foreign missions, embassies, and consulates at home. These skills, knowledge, and power to engage demonstrate CSOs' leaders' competencies, as Çitaku and Ramadani (2020) discuss. They are also capable of playing a role in preparing and promoting the rights of the marginalised, victims, and young people in civic engagement, change, and development processes despite social, economic, and political constraints, shifts and restrictions. CSO leaders in the Occupied Palestinian Territories, such as in the Gaza Strip, for example, showed an exceptional style of leadership while adapting and challenging their lack of funding, political constraints, and deadlock, and adhering to lockdown policies imposed by local authorities to save lives, as Natil (2021, 2020: 9–17) discusses.

Some CSOs run awareness campaigns, dialogue and discussions through social media to discuss the mechanisms of participation in decision-making, the role of the media, the empowerment of women, and the promotion of human rights and community peacebuilding despite the lockdown; in particular, discusses Palestinian media discourse and engagement. There have been a number of CSO leaders, such as those of the SVF in Palestine, who have motivated their staff and volunteers to work from home and engage actively with their society and target groups over the internet (Amer, 2021). The SVF continued working with marginalised and vulnerable groups of women in wider society to run local activities to defy and challenge the shifts, hoping for and seeking a better life. CSOs engage through social media platforms like Zoom and Facebook, and they continue to run some online sessions to raise awareness about fighting violence against women and to provide psychological and social support sessions for children who are in need of playtime, having fun and carrying out some activities in the pandemic. This has encouraged some donors, such as the Canada Feminism Fund, to engage with CSOs, as Fida Amer says:

> This project aimed at empowering young leaders as agents for activism and organisational engagement in the Gaza Strip. SVF developed the capacities of 150 young leaders aged 20-30 years old in fighting against domestic violence against women to contribute to a state of conflict transformation within society. SVF's project considered solid risk mitigation strategies for the safe and effective delivery of programming in the context of the COVID-19 pandemic in accordance with WHO guidelines and instructions.
>
> (Amer, 2021)

Despite the challenges to the culture of society, political structures, CSOs' leadership of local activism, and grassroots groups, women still fight for full rights in their societies by engaging in political, social, and civil issues and responsibilities (Jad, 2018; Natil, 2021). However, the question of sustainability is a challenging issue for many CSO leaders. Raweh (in Chapter 10) has discussed local Yemeni CSOs that are currently working in the field of conflict resolution and peacebuilding activities in an attempt to answer the research question of whether local Yemeni CSOs have had effective leadership during the period of conflict. Do they have strategic plans and financial sustainability? Have they investigated their current capacities and challenges? Raweh also attempted to work out the percentage of CSOs that have a strategic plan and the kind of financial sustainability mechanisms they use by answering those questions. The research also proposes recommendations for more effective leadership and the kind of support needed to enhance the working practice of the Yemeni CSOs in an attempt to enrich the literature with accurate assessments and opportunities for support and partnership with a wide range of stakeholders.

## References

Amer, F. (2021). Interview with society voice foundation director, 14 September 2021.
Bennis, W. (2007). The challenge of leadership in the modern world: Introduction to special issue. *American Psychologist*, *62*, 2–5.
Çitaku, F., & Ramadani, H. (2020). Leadership competency model-drenica: Generalizability of leadership competencies. *International Journal of Organizational Leadership*, *9*, 156–162.

Çitaku, F., Violato, C., Beran, T., Donnon, T., Hecker, K., & Cawthorpe, D. (2012). Leadership competencies for medical education and healthcare professions: Population-based study. *BMJ Open*, *2*, e000812. https://doi.org/10.1136/bmjopen-2012-000812.

Cosgrove, S. (2010). *Leadership from the margins: Women and civil society organisations in Argentina*. Rutgers University Press.

Estrada, C., & Carranza, M. (2016). Leadership style in nonprofit organizations, the Mexican case. *International Journal of Business, Humanities and Technology*, *6*(4), 25–32.

Fowler, A., & Malunga, C. (2020). *NGO management*. Routledge.

Graham, L. (2016). *Beyond social capital: The role of leadership, trust and government policy in Northern Ireland's victim support groups*. Palgrave Macmillan.

Hudson, M. (2017). *Manging without profit: Leadership, governance and management of civil society organisations*. Directory of Social Change.

Jad, I. (2007). NGOs: Between buzzwords and social movements. *Development in Practice*, *17*(4–5), 622–629. https://doi.org/10.1080/09614520701469781.

Jad, I. (2018). *The Palestinian women's activism: Nationalism, secularism and Islamism*. Syracuse University Press.

Lewis, D. (2014). *Non-governmental organisations, management and development* (3rd ed.). Routledge.

McMullin, C., & Raggo, P. (2020). Leadership and governance in times of crisis: A balancing act for non-profit boards. *Nonprofit and Voluntary Sector Quarterly*, *49*(6), 1182–1190. https://doi.org/10.1177/0899764020964582.

Natil, I. (2020). Introducing barriers to effective civil society organisations. In I. Natil, V. Malila, & Y. Sai (Eds.), *Barriers to effective civil society organisations: Political, social and financial shifts*. Routledge, 1–8.

Natil, N. (2021). *Conflict, civil society, and women's empowerment: Insights from the West Bank and the Gaza Strip*. Emerald Publishing.

# 3 Four-pillars Approach to Effective Management and Leadership

## Humanitarian Aid and Development Assistance CSOs

*Mahmoud Almadhoun*

**Introduction**

CSOs have been facing great scrutiny over the past decade for their allegedly inefficient and underdeveloped managerial and organisational structure which resulted in a waste of resources. Some scholars argue that due to the lack of a driving force for survival that pushes for innovation in the private sector (Bradley et al., 2003), CSOs fail to, and lack the desire to, innovate in their organisational and operational and managerial structure. Increasingly Arab CSOs leaders are facing complex managerial problems as organisations are playing a more significant role in the regional arena of humanitarian aid. Even though many scholars have shed light on the increasing importance of the role individual leaders play in the success of a CSO (Fowler, 1997; Kelleher & McLaren, 1996; Smillie & Hailey, 2001), there has been a great gap in the actual research into the formulation of effective leadership and managerial programmes (Heiley & James, 2004).

CSOs developed initiatives to improve management capacity and support good leadership practices within the sector such as Harvard Humanitarian Initiative, Core Humanitarian Standard Alliance (CHS Alliance), Start Network, Learning in CSOs (LICSOs), and Active Learning Network for Accountability & Performance (ALNAP). Initiatives stress the importance of management and leadership for the CSOs within the humanitarian aid and development assistance sector (Almadhoun, 2021).

In this chapter, based on an extensive literature review and the professional-managerial experience in the field of humanitarian work, the author puts forward an approach to establish the meaning of management and leadership that includes four pillars which must be considered by the CSOs to achieve the organisational results more effectively and efficiently.

DOI: 10.4324/9781003288145-3

## Importance of Good Management and Leadership in a CSO

Given the growth in the humanitarian aid sector, the organisational size and the complexity of compliance requirements have expanded significantly, which put more pressure on the CSOs to continuously improve their management systems and leadership qualities to meet the expectations of key stakeholders in a challenging landscape. To cope, CSOs need to develop policies and procedures to better manage to be able to identify the management problems, issues related to budgeting and financial planning, risk management, and risk mitigation, poor-fundraising management, problems in governance and the roles of boards, and problems in human resources management.

In order to achieve this within the humanitarian and development context, the Core Humanitarian Standard on Quality and Accountability (CHS) set nine commitments that all humanitarian actors involved in planning, managing, or implementing a humanitarian response, including staff and volunteers of local, national, and international agencies can use to improve the quality and effectiveness of the assistance they provide. One of these nine commitments (commitment Nr. 8) stresses the importance of leadership and people management by asserting that: 'communities and people affected by crisis receive the assistance they require from competent and well-managed staff and volunteers, who are supported to do their job effectively, and are treated fairly and equitably.'

The four pillars are as follows: strategy and organisational development, leadership and human resources, managing relations with key stakeholders, and mobilisation of funds, sustainability, and innovation management.

## Pillar 1: Strategy and Organisational Development

CSOs differ in their objectives and the type of environment in which they operate (Walsh & Lenihan, 2006). Some operate in relatively stable environments while others operate in war zones trying to provide basic lifesaving. For a CSO's strategy to be successful, it must be able to draw a clear picture of the direction and the scale of its operations, providing a long-term vision to satisfy internal and external stakeholders. The strategy must include a flexible and dynamic financial and operational plan showing the CSO's ability to match available resources with ongoing and future operations effectively and efficiently. It should consider the natural volatility of the work environment the CSO usually operates in (Johnson & Scholes, 1993).

When devising a strategic plan, it must go through multiple essential stages to reach maturity: starting with environmental analysis, then to strategy formulation and implementation, and ending with strategy evaluation (Aboramadan, 2018). CSOs need to link vision, mission, and values together and formulate a strategic plan to turn strategy into programmes. With environmental analysis, management must conduct comprehensive research into the environment in which they are going to carry out their operations. Virtually all CSO operations are carried out in developing countries that have fragile economic, political, and institutional structures (Walsh & Lenihan, 2006). It is essential for CSOs to employ a participatory approach to leadership. Employees (including volunteers) have crucial field knowledge that can play a major role in understanding the technicalities and the realities of the fieldwork. Management must simultaneously create supporting policies that aim to maintain the projects in the long run once they are up and running, ensuring continuous benefit from the projects to both donors and aid-receivers while maintaining organisation stability.

The strategy must be based on an understanding of the needs and expectations of both internal and external stakeholders. It must be based on understanding internal capabilities. Furthermore, supporting policies must be developed, reviewed, and updated to ensure the programmes and organisational sustainability. Strategy and supporting policies must be communicated and deployed through action plans and processes. This pillar requires a participatory approach of leadership.

## Likert System 4 Method for Organisational Development

Likert System 4 is an organisational development tool developed by Rensis Likert. He outlined four systems of management to describe the relationship, involvement, and roles of managers and subordinates. The management systems, established by Likert, include 'Exploitative Authoritative (System I), Benevolent Authoritative (System II), Consultative (System III), and Participative (System IV).' Likert's Organisational Profile Survey can be recommended here for CSOs to measure organisational productivity and change over time. The four management systems mentioned in the Likert method provide the whole structure of the organisational profile survey. The fourth system, participative, is described as the ideal system for human-concerned organisations. In this system, leadership has confidence in its staff, personnel at all levels feel real responsibility for organisational goals, there is strong communication, and a substantial amount of cooperative teamwork.

## Pillar 2: Leadership and Human Resources

Human resource management is a foundational component of any CSO. Effective HRM is especially important in the humanitarian sector as it plays an essential role in the effectiveness of CSOs' operations (Guo et al., 2011). Employees are an organisation's most valuable assets as they are the reflection of the CSO's mission that makes its vision turn into a reality (Aboramadan, 2018). HRM includes recruitment, deployment, governance, legal management, compliance with international and local laws, organisational culture development and deployment, training and retention, preservation of company values and ethics, dispute management, and employee management.

Trends show that CSOs employees are easily replaceable in local communities which consequently leads to low HR investment (Bryant & Allen, 2009; Lepak & Snell, 2002) as mentioned early on (Smillie, 1999,1995). There has been a great waste of talent and spirit of volunteers and employees in CSOs, especially locals, from the inefficient, careless, and sometimes unethical management of employees and resources. This could explain the high employee turnover, especially talented ones in leadership positions (Civicus, 2002). Management must put innovation in HR as a core objective as it aims to tackle HR-related problems in the humanitarian sector. Harvard Humanitarian Initiative provides proactive practical recommendations for solving some of the main HR issues many scholars have pointed out in the literature as follows:

**Training programmes and staff motivation**: Many of the training programmes, including leadership programmes, provided in the humanitarian aid industry are static, curriculum-based programmes that are usually given over the span of days or, at most, two weeks. HR should aim at providing modern, effective, and rejuvenating training programmes to all its staff. These training initiatives must aim at spreading and enforcing the organisational culture to strengthen the employee-organisation relationship and trust. They must prepare employees to be dynamic and flexible to organisational and environmental changes. They must bring social and cultural awareness into the office and the field, especially to employees and volunteers who work with foreign cultures, to build up soft and hard skills that can increase employee values. This must aim at increasing employee participation through building employee confidence and satisfaction, especially for field employees and volunteers where taking initiative and being proactive is essential for the success of projects. Management and leadership training initiatives must be provided for the managers and high-performance employees as well as increasing management competency and providing the resources needed for new talent to emerge. Staff motivation must also be at the top of the HRM list. Creating and maintaining a clear reward-and-benefit system that keeps employees engaged and rewarded is crucial for maintaining productivity, especially on a day-to-day basis.

**Recruitment criteria**: HR is leading the recruitment of employees and volunteers. This puts the responsibility of hiring managers in the hands of the HRM. Recruitment must prioritise both hard and soft skills when making a decision. HR must scan potential candidates for their social principles and personal values. Recruiting employees that are already accustomed to the company's culture and are in line with the organisation strategy are more likely to be more loyal, productive, and proactive and are more likely to stay for a long period of time. This brings the crucial task of making internal career progression clear and possible for aspiring employees, and for ensuring there are promotional non-managerial positions for talented technical staff who are not capable of holding managerial positions.

**Policy and complaints**: HRM is responsible for the formulation of security and safety policies and the code of conduct, then integrating them into the organisational culture and strategy. The code of conduct must address workplace ethics covering areas on the prevention of workplace harassment, sexual exploitation and abuse, behavioural misconducts, racism, unfair treatment, etc., and must clearly state the punishment for breaking the rules. Staff must be made fully aware of these policies and guidelines, making it clear that they are to be followed during and outside the job. Breaking those guidelines at any time must result in punishment and immediate termination to ensure a safe, secure, and fair work environment and any code of conduct complaints must be dealt with in a timely manner. Employee and community complaints are also a rich source of information that can aid in improving operations and bringing innovation and efficiency. These complaints must be given high regard, as they are an indication of the efficiency and effectiveness of the organisation. It is important to mention that research into HRM systems and methods in the humanitarian sector is still in its early stages (Akingbola, 2012) due to a lack of investment in this arena. Leadership, management, and the HR team must think very creatively and innovatively and take initiative, thinking outside the box in the aim of tackling strategic obstacles.

**Leadership**: Empirical evidence (Conger & Kanugo, 1987) shows that leaders play a primary role in developing, shaping, and maintaining the organisation's culture and pushing through innovation in an organisation. Organisational culture is defined as a set of values, expectations, and methodologies drawn by the organisation to help guide its operations and future decisions (Reiman & Oedewald, 2002). Alvesson (2002) found a direct relationship between organisational culture and performance, highlighting the importance of dynamic culture that can help the organisation and its employees adapt to any given situation. Brown and Covey (1987) and Aboramadan (2018) carried out extensive research on the leadership practices essential to shaping organisational culture and organisation management systems. Lowder (2007) has formalised five pillars of effective leadership, which are all essential for managers to be aware of as they shape all human interaction taking place within the organisation and outside of it. These pillars will be discussed briefly to provide a simple outline of expected traits and behaviours CSOs must aspire to have (Covey, 1990; Crosby, 1992, Manz & Sims Jr., 1990; McIntosh & Rima, 1997; Peters & Watermen Jr., 1982; Quinn, 1996, 2005; Tichy & Sherman, 1994; Waterman Jr., 1987).

**Personal effectiveness**: These personal attributes are usually developed in the early life of the leader. They are essential in the long run for ensuring positive managerial outcomes and psychological stability. Examples of these traits are 'individual trustworthiness, strong ethical system, tough-mindedness, personal optimism, self-motivated, goal-oriented, focused on important issues, works toward self-improvement, sets priorities setting, and uses effective time management' (Covey, 1990; Crosby, 1992; Quinn, 1996, 2005; Tichy & Sherman, 1994; Waterman Jr., 1987, Lowder, 2007). Through time, these traits manifest themselves in the organisation, increasing staff and organisational effectiveness and efficiency.

**Interpersonal relationship effectiveness**: This pillar takes a deeper look into the virtues, rather than traits, that play a major role in the motives and philosophies behind the personal traits of the managers. These virtues include 'trust, compassion, empathy, fairness, objectivity, encouragement, guiding, and motivating' (Covey, 1990; Crosby, 1992; Manz & Sims Jr., 1990; Quinn, 1996, 2005; Tichy & Sherman, 1994; Waterman Jr., 1987). In the humanitarian sector, managers must demonstrate and apply the humanitarian principles set by the EU Commission and UN which are of humanity, neutrality, imperiality, and operational independence in all their decisions and actions. This pillar is of extreme importance because research suggests that leaders who score high in this pillar have a very high potential in affecting the behavioural pattern and decisions of others around them. Leaders with these traits must satisfy the humanitarian principles and must be examined closely as selfish and manipulative leaders might take advantage of their position for personal benefit (McIntosh & Rima, 1997; Takala, 2005).

**Managerial effectiveness**: This plays an essential role in determining the effectiveness of the management in leading the organisation and its employees forward, playing a role in the effectiveness in the implementation of organisation policy. Behavioural traits associated with this pillar include 'team spirit, achieves productivity through people, delegates authority, empowers others, communication at all organizational pillars, demonstrate candor, seeks continuous organizational improvement maintains a bias for organizational action, and emulates high organizational values' (Covey, 1990; Crosby, 1992; Manz & Sims Jr., 1990; Quinn, 1996, 2005; Tichy & Sherman, 1994; Waterman Jr., 1987). These traits increase in importance as the size of the CSO increases, needing its managers and employees to work effectively in many different cultures and environments. This pillar is parallel to the importance of deploying effective managerial control systems, as managers that show managerial effectiveness competence can fully utilise the managerial control systems, resulting in the successful achievement of organisational goals and objectives.

**Operational effectiveness**: This evaluates the success of the manager in running the day-to-day and large-scale operations of the organisation. Factors like net profit, statistics of successful operations, effective aid delivery, and financial management efficiency are used to evaluate managers in this pillar (Lowder, 2006).

**Societal effectiveness**: This evaluates the manager's impact and influence on external stakeholders such as governments, donors, local communities, and suppliers. It evaluates the level of genuine humane focus of management over social objectives such as equality, gender equality, race equality, environmental sustainability, etc. Managers who demonstrate strong involvement with the external environment can positively impact the operations of the CSO, especially when working with weak governments that rely on personal relationships. CSOs tend to aim, intentionally and unintentionally, at employing the 'hot-shot' charismatic leaders that lack the professional-managerial skills and vision needed to develop the organisational structure and managerial system (Bryman, 1992; Edwards, 1999; Smillie & Hailey, 2001; Ahmad, 2000; Lewis, 2003, 2001). If the management fails to align structure strategy and organisational vision into the management system, the organisation and its employees will be negatively impacted in the long run (Lowder, 2006) resulting in the downfall of the CSO. This links back to (Hailey & James, 2004) the concept of leadership as a relationship rather than a person. Leaders must be both managerial in the professionalism, etiquette, and rationality of managing the CSO's operation and must be value-driven and ambitious, acting as role models for employees, as an inspiration to the organisation's culture and as trustworthy and reliable leaders to external stakeholders.

Management is responsible for forming the culture based on a dynamic and adaptive set of values and virtues through establishing regulatory guidelines to be followed by the management and leadership, employees, and the CSO as a whole. These regulatory guidelines must be easily accessible to all stakeholders and employees and they must reflect the mission, vision, and values of the organisation. Management and leaders are responsible for applying these guidelines into their work ethics and their life, serving as role models to the employees and other organisations. With much of the research conducted on the role of leadership in organisations being based on the private sector with little focus on the non-profit or public sector (Adair, 2002; Bennis & Nanus, 2004; Kotter, 1996).

Management must always be ready to adapt and change based on the volatile environment it operates in. These virtue-based guidelines are built on being 'interpretive.' As argued, principles followed in the humanitarian sector are made to be interpreted in the most positive and suitable way based on the situation the humanitarian is in. Measuring CSOs performance is of extreme importance to external and internal stakeholders as performance provides grounds for holding the CSO accountable for resources and funds spent on its business operations and its projects, and to help measure the CSO's impact on the external environment (Beamon, 2004, O'Dwyer & Uerman, 2008). Scholars have agreed that measuring performance in a CSO is extremely complex (Sawhill & Williamson, 2001; Speckbacher, 2003; Micheli & Kennerly, 2005), which is why management control systems can be used to aid managers in evaluating the management process and the CSO's performance.

Management control is a crucial factor in defining, monitoring, and reviewing management systems. Anthony (1965) defines management control as the process used by managers to ensure effective and efficient use of resources in the operations of the organisation. Management control involves managing internal stakeholders and managing relationships with external stakeholders and the outside environment, all while keeping track of the organisation's operations (Ahmed, 2014). Management is responsible for maintaining these systems to high standards, all while being ready to carry out any modifications to the system in the event of sudden change or crisis. Management is also responsible for the translation of the data gathered by the management control systems into tangible and objective and transparent performance indexes that can be presented to external stakeholders through financial statements or other means.

It is important to point out that most CSOs focus on reporting project performance while they ignore or poorly report management performance (Ramadan & Borgonovi, 2015). This is why it is crucial that management be able to combine the use of organisational culture to set out clear and tangible objectives, while at the same time use management control systems to collect and analyse data, producing comprehensive financial, organisational, and managerial performance analysis which can be used not only to state the accountability requirements of stakeholders but also as a tool for the managers themselves to increase efficiency and effectiveness of their management, allowing for better resource management and insight into creating a more dynamic, adaptive, and innovative managerial function (Poister, 2003; Aboramadan, 2018).

## Pillar 3: Managing Relations with Key Stakeholders

As discussed in the pillar 2 section, the managers who hold the leadership traits introduced by Lowder (2007) tend to be charismatic and social, playing an essential role in building relationships with external stakeholders, especially in areas where personal relations prevail over professional ones, which is very common in the humanitarian sector.

## Pillar 4: Mobilisation of Funds, Sustainability, and Innovation Management

Organisational excellence in this field can only be achieved through excellent financial management. Keating and Frumkin (2000, 2001) provide empirical evidence that links the ability of an organisation to translate its accounting decisions and financial information to its external stakeholders to maintain long-term fund sustainability. Whether it is the grant-making organisation, local governments, or auditing teams, the management must have the ability to produce transparent and easy-to-read financial statements that clearly display the effectiveness of the CSO's operation and truly reflect its culture and vision. It is management's task to deploy internal control measures that verify the authenticity of the accounting and financial data produced, allowing management itself and external stakeholders to gauge the success of managerial policies and organisational strategies (Herman & Rez, 1999).

## Conclusion

Literature suggests that managers and leaders in CSOs often lack the financial knowledge and experience needed to run these delegated financial tasks effectively (Inglis, 1997b; Aboramadan, 2018). It is essential for management to carry out a full assessment of the competency of the accounting and financial department, and, if needed, invest in recruiting a professional consultancy and financial contract (Kaplan, 1996). CSOs' management and leadership mechanisms, competencies, and tools are not only important but also crucial for the CSOs in the humanitarian aid and development assistance context. This argument contributes to a better understanding of the management and leadership roles in the humanitarian aid and development assistance sector, while focusing on four pillars of good management and leadership practices, which will serve as a guide for maximising the efficiency, effectiveness, and impact of the humanitarian aid and development assistance programmes designed and implemented by the CSOs.

## References

Aboramadan, M. (2018). CSOs management: A roadmap to effective practices. *Journal of Global Responsibility*, *9*(4), 372–387.

Adair, J. (2002). *Effective strategic leadership*. Macmillan.

Ahmad, M. M. (2000). *Donors, CSOs, the state and their clients in Bangladesh*. The Arkleton Trust (UK).

Akingbola, K. (2012). A model of strategic nonprofit human resource management. *Voluntas: International Journal of Voluntary and Nonprofit Organizations*, *24*(1), 1–27.

Almadhoun, M. (2021). Praktische Umsetzung des core humanitarian standard on quality and accountability (CHS). In M. Heuser & T. Abdelalem (Eds.), *Internationale Herausforderungen humanitärer NGOs*. Springer Gabler. https://doi.org/10.1007/978-3-662-62494-4_8.

Alvesson, M. (2002). *Understanding organisational culture*. SAGE Publications.

Anthony, R. N. (1965). *Planning and control systems: A framework for analysis*. Harvard University Press.

Beamon, B. M. (2004). Humanitarian relief chains: Issues and challenges, Proceedings of the 34th International Conference on Computers and Industrial Engineering, San Francisco, CA, November, pp. 14–16.

Bennis, W., & Nanus, B. (2004). *Leaders*. HarperCollins.

Bradley, B., Jansen, P., & Silverman, L. (2003). The nonprofit sector's $100 billion opportunity. *Harvard Business Review*, *81*, 94–103.

Brown, D., & Covey, J. G. (1987). Development organizations and organization development: Towards an expanded paradigm for organization development. *Research in Organizational Change and Development*, *1*, 59–87.

Bryant, P. C., & Allen, D. G. (2009). Emerging organizations' characteristics as predictors of human capital employment mode: A theoretical perspective. *Human Resource Management Review*, *19*, 347–355.

Bryman, A. (1992). *Charisma and leadership in organisations*. Sage.

CIVICUS. (2002). *Connecting civil society worldwide*, newsletter No 175 August, Johannesburg.
Conger, J. A., & Kanungo, R. N. (1987). Toward a behavioral theory of charismatic leadership in organizational settings. *Academy of Management Review, 12*(4), 6376–6347.
Covey, S. R. (1990). *Principle-centered leadership*. Fireside.
Crosby, P. B. (1992). *Completeness, quality in the 21st century*. Plume.
Edwards, M. (1999). CSO performance: What breeds success? *World Development, 27*(2), 1361–1374.
Fowler, A. (1997). *Striking a balance: A guide to enhancing the effectiveness of non-governmental organisations in international development*. Earthscan.
Frumkin, P., & Keating, E. K. (2001). The price of doing good: Executive compensation in nonprofit organizations. *SSRN Electronic Journal*. Published.
Guo, C., Brown, W. A., Ashcraft, R. F., Yoshioka, C. F., & Dong, H.-K. D. (2011). Strategic human resources management in nonprofit organizations. *Review of Public Personnel Administration, 31*, 248–269.
Hailey, J., & James, R. (2004). 'Trees die from the top?': International perspectives on CSO leadership development. *Voluntas: International Journal of Voluntary and Nonprofit Organizations*, (4), 343–353.
Herman, R. D., & Renz, D. O. (1999). Theses on nonprofit organizational effectiveness. *Nonprofit and Voluntary Sector Quarterly, 28*(2), 107–126.
Inglis, S. (1997b). Shared leadership in the governance of amateur sport: Perceptions of executive directors and volunteer board members. *Avante, 3*(1), 14–33.
Johnson, G., & Scholes, K. (1993). *Exploring corporate strategy* (3rd ed.). Prentice-Hall.
Kaplan, A. (1996). *The development practitioner's handbook*. Pluto Press.
Keating, E., & Frumkin, P. (2000). Reengineering nonprofit financial accountability: Toward a more reliable foundation for regulation. *Public Administration Review, 63*(1), 3–15.
Kelleher, D., & McLaren, K. (1996). *Grabbing the tiger by the tail: CSO learning for organisational change*. Canadian Council for International Cooperation.
Kotter, J. (1996). *Leading change*. Harvard Business School Press.
Lepak, D. P., & Snell, S. A. (2002). Examining the human resource architecture: The relationships among human capital, employment, and human resource configurations. *Journal of Management, 28*, 517–543.
Lewis, D. (2001). *The management of non-governmental development organisations*. Routledge.
Lewis, D. (2003). Theorizing the organization and management of non-governmental development organizations. *Public Management Review, 5*(3), 325–344.
Manz, C. C., & Sims Jr., H. P. (1990). *Super-leadership*. Berkley.
McIntosh, G. L., & Rima, S. D., Sr. (1997). *Overcoming the dark side of leadership: The paradox of personal dysfunction*. Baker Books.
Micheli, P., & Kennerly, M. (2005). Performance measurement frameworks in public and non profit sectors. *Production Planning and Control, 16*(2), 125–134.

O'Dwyer, B., & Unerman, J. (2008). The paradox of greater CSO accountability: A case study. *Accounting, Organizations and Society, 33*, 801–824.

Peters, T. J., & Watermen Jr., R. H. (1982). *In search of excellence.* Warner Books.

Poister, T. H. (2003). *Measuring performance in public and nonprofit organizations.* Jossey-Bass.

Quinn, R. E. (1996). *Deep change: Discovering the leader within.* Jossey-Bass.

Quinn, R. E. (2005). Moments of greatness. *Harvard Business Review, 83*(7/8), 74–83.

Ramadan, M. A., & Borgonovi, E. (2015). Performance measurement and management in non governmental organizations. *Journal of Business and Management, 17*(2), 70–76.

Reiman, T., & Oedewald, P. (2002). The assessment of organizational culture: A methodological study. www.vtt.fi/inf/pdf/tiedotteet/2002/T2140.pdf.

Sawhill, J. C., & Williamson, D. (2001). Mission impossible? Measuring success in nonprofit organizations. *Nonprofit Management and Leadership, 11*(3), 371–386.

Smillie, I. (1995). *The Almas Bazar: Altruism under fire – Non-profit organisations and international development.* Intermediate Technology Publications.

Smillie, I. (1999). Public support and the politics of aid. *Development, 42*(3), 71–76.

Smillie, I., & Hailey, J. (2001). *Managing for change: Leadership, strategy and management in Asian CSO.* Earthscan.

Speckbacher, G. (2003). The economics of performance management in nonprofit organizations. *Nonprofit Management and Leadership, 13*(3), 267–281.

Takala, T. (2005). Charismatic leadership and power. *Problems & Perspectives in Management, 3*(3), 45–57.

Tichy, N. M., & Sherman, S. (1994). *Control your own destiny or someone else will.* Harper Business.

Walsh, E., & Lenihan, H. (2006). Accountability and effectiveness of CSOs: Adapting business tools successfully. *Development in Practice, 16*(5), 412–424.

Waterman Jr., R. H. (1987). *The renewal factor.* Bantam.

# 4 CSOs Leaders between Covid-19 and Technology Platforms

## Peacebuilding Case Study

*Bassam Kassoumeh*

## Introduction

This chapter explores the implications of using technology and online tools, such as Zoom, Skype, and recently Clubhouse, to conduct peacebuilding dialogue on marginalised and neglected groups during the Covid-19 pandemic. The pandemic, which has forced CSOs to move peacebuilding dialogue to online and virtual spaces, offered new opportunities for the inclusion of typically marginalised and conflict-affected groups in peacebuilding activities.

The improved inclusion of conflict-affected people in peacebuilding dialogue through digital platforms offers new opportunities for conducive peace and reconciliation (Leonardsson & Rudd, 2015). The pandemic has also pushed the localisation agenda and enforced the systems change, giving more power and autonomy to CSOs to design and implement their own projects, as international non-governmental organisations (INGOs) are no longer on the ground due to travel restrictions brought about by the pandemic (Conducive Space for Peace, 2020, 2021). The pandemic has also forced grassroots CSOs to adopt new leadership strategies to adapt to the new operating model.

However, the use of technology by CSOs can potentially amplify the marginalisation of groups without access to the internet and technology, which risks the domination of peacebuilding dialogue by certain classes. This domination could reinforce elite capture, impede meaningful participation, and exacerbate conflict rather than contribute to peace.

In pursuit of addressing this knowledge gap, this chapter takes a micro-level approach to peacebuilding, which receives little attention, by working closely with peacebuilding CSO leaders, and building on the widely available macro-level peacebuilding literature that focuses on formal negotiations (Saunders, 1999).

DOI: 10.4324/9781003288145-4

This chapter is structured as follows. First, the chapter will provide an updated summary of the advantages of using technology to conduct peacebuilding activities. Then the chapter will define online peacebuilding dialogue. The chapter will then summarise the adverse effects of using technology for peacebuilding dialogue, and the absence of INGOs on the ground, with examples from Syria and Yemen. Finally, the chapter will then present different leadership theories that may help CSO leaders in ensuring inclusive and meaningful participation, and address and minimise any potential marginalisation, power imbalances, and leadership biases brought about by the use of technology during the Covid-19 pandemic and beyond.

## Methodology

To overcome issues of limited access due to the pandemic and due to the nature of the research, a Participatory Action Research (PAR) methodology is chosen to expand and improve the current knowledge and understanding of the challenges faced by CSO leaders, in their contexts, when conducting OPD. PAR relies on the co-production of knowledge by involving those affected by these challenges, which can potentially result in an action for a better outcome (Kemmis & McTaggart, 2005; Mckay, 2011; Beaton et al., 2017). In contrast, traditional research methodologies often force those affected by the research to relinquish control to the researcher, resulting in distorted and less accurate problem identification (Cornwall & Jewkes, 1995; Guzman et al., 2016). Interviews with Yemeni and Syrian CSO leaders were conducted by using online tools, in addition to a questionnaire circulated to peacebuilding leaders in both contexts.

## Online Peacebuilding Dialogue

Due to the pandemic, CSOs were forced to move their peacebuilding dialogue to online platforms to avoid the collapse of peacebuilding work and reduce conflicts and tensions between communities. The reliance on online tools has improved the participation in peacebuilding activities in some contexts by allowing remote, marginalised, and disadvantaged groups to join and participate in peacebuilding dialogue (Kassoumeh, 2020; Alberti & Clark, 2020). Consequently, CSO participation and influence have increased as OPD paved the way for genuine peacebuilding on a local and grassroots level (Edes & Garrison, 2021; ibid.). This chapter, thus, defines online peacebuilding dialogue (OPD) as 'the dialogic process between conflicting parties with different and opposing perspectives that allows the development of genuine and sustainable peace through an online virtual safe space' (Kassoumeh, 2020: 93).

The increased connectivity which resulted in the development of powerful online communities is reshaping the citizen-state social contract, providing opportunities for building more equitable societies (Peace Direct, 2020). In contrast, prior to the pandemic, representatives of international CSOs typically used to speak on behalf of those marginalised in meetings as these groups are not able to travel and attend. Similarly, international-led peace initiatives often lacked a systematic approach for the inclusion of local actors and are mostly focused on the problem rather than people which often results in interventions that are not conflict-sensitive and with limited buy-in from the targeted community as opposed to locally led initiatives.

## Adverse Effect of Using Digital Tools on Peacebuilding

While the digitalisation of peacebuilding work can create leverage for peace by enabling marginalised groups to join peacebuilding meetings, it can also potentially add new layers of conflict (FriEnt, 2021). For example, digital and online tools can amplify the marginalisation of other disadvantaged groups within these marginalised groups especially those who reside in areas with poor internet penetration (Alberti & Clark, 2020). Further, it is thought that the lack of technological equipment, poor infrastructures, and low digital literacy amongst these disadvantaged groups are principally the biggest challenges to their true and effective digital participation (Peace Direct, 2020). Participants argue that even prior to the pandemic, rural women, refugees, and internally displaced people, especially those who are illiterate, are amongst those who are most marginalised from peace talks in Yemen and Syria (Helmi 2021; Mashhour, 2021). The pandemic has, thus, widened the urban/rural divide in some contexts which could contribute to additional biases (Bell et al., 2020).

In Syria, in addition to electricity cuts, government internet access restrictions and surveillance are amongst the biggest challenges in ensuring a safe space for genuine and inclusive digital participation. Similarly, in Yemen, participants with bad internet connections are forcibly put on mute to avoid the disruption of dialogues. OPD participants have also reported Zoom fatigue, and participation is seen to be declining especially as some meetings end with no clear outcome (Edes & Garrison, 2021; Aladwar, 2021).

Adding to this, in both contexts, there has been an increased use of 'Clubhouse' – an invitation-only drop-in audio chat app (Mac Observer, 2021). The app offers a free and safe alternative virtual discussion space in times where people cannot meet in person due to the pandemic or in highly authoritarian contexts. Political discussions and topics currently dominate the app, while peacebuilders are using it extensively to conduct peacebuilding dialogue (Bangkok Post, 2021). However, Clubhouse is labelled as 'elitist' as the app is exclusively available by invitation and to iPhone users (Mac Observer, 2021). This inherently excludes those with lower incomes since iPhones are not widely available and cost more than other smartphones.

Consequently, those with superior digital capacities hold a new form of power to dominate OPDs as they are better positioned to join decision-making online meetings, replicating, and reinforcing power imbalances (International Alert, 2020; Peace Direct, 2020; Edes & Garrison, 2021). The marginalisation of such groups reinforces elite capture, hampers meaningful participation, and potentially creates new grievances or exacerbates current ones, adding another layer to the conflict (Bickmore, 2014).

## Absence of INGOs on the Ground

Similarly, while systems change initiatives that empower local actors in peacebuilding and gives them more ownership, legitimacy and flexibility have been pushed for by international INGOs for years, these initiatives have not been conducive to creating an enabling environment for locally led peacebuilding initiatives. Furthermore, these systems change initiatives did not lead to broader systems transformation, especially as funding channelling mechanisms have not activated accountability systems and the role for change agents, such as leaders, is often overlooked (Conducive Space for Peace, 2021).

However, during the pandemic, the absence of INGOs on the ground due to travel restrictions has highlighted the role of locally led peacebuilding and CSO leadership as these organisations are now at the frontline of peacebuilding (Conducive Space for Peace, 2020). This has also accelerated the localisation agenda, and some of these local actors, including CSOs, and marginalised groups are able to represent themselves in virtual spaces and actively participate in peacebuilding dialogue (Edes & Garrison, 2021). Moreover, CSOs are now playing a bigger role of bridging various levels of peacebuilding, as they are both active on the ground and involved in Track one peace negotiations.

## Leaders and Biases

However, the absence of INGOs on the ground is not always beneficial as the reduced oversight and accountability is causing CSO leadership biases. For example, while conducting interviews and surveys, leadership biases and accountability issues were raised by participants. While CSOs are increasingly focusing and targeting their activities on marginalised groups to address participation issues, participant selection biases amongst leaders, which are common in peacebuilding activities, are replicated in online platforms (Hirschmann & Doesum, 2021). In Yemen, CSOs are becoming increasingly decentralised and fractured, lacking upward accountability and prioritising certain groups while marginalising others, especially from the opposition (Mansour, 2021).

In Yemen, CSOs occasionally lack feedback mechanisms for reporting issues of marginalisation and meaningful participation resulting in accountability issues. CSO leaders are addressing this marginalisation by adopting feedback mechanisms like post-event surveys and close and regular communication with local coordinators and participants to flag any potential inclusion issues. That said, leaders confirmed that these measures on their own are insufficient.

In order to maximise the benefits and minimise the adverse effects, participants highlighted the need for improved leadership skills that could advance their capacities to ensure equitable participation, reduce biases, and improve accountability in online settings. Additionally, as online spaces become more complex, such as Clubhouse, this necessitates the significance of advanced moderation and facilitation skills to ensure meaningful participation.

The following section will aim to explore and summarise leadership theories and identify an understanding of leadership in CSOs that addresses and minimises issues surrounding inclusion and marginalisation in OPD.

## Leadership

Whilst research on leadership is a complicated process given the complexity and inexhaustibility of available theories and conceptualisations, this chapter relies on Robbins's definition of leadership as the utilisation of influence, deliberation, and communication to motivate followers to achieve collective goals (Fredendall et al., 2001). Furthermore, this chapter defines leaders as those implementing peacebuilding activities, regardless of their management level, such as peacebuilding dialogue facilitators or community leaders.

Accordingly, leadership in CSOs is more than simply occupying an institutional position but rather the ability to mobilise others and guide a process of social change through participation and engagement. This is essential for peacebuilding CSOs, as the prevention of violent conflict requires inclusive peacebuilding, local leadership, and engagement that traditional leadership theories fail to emphasise. This chapter will present leadership theories that are relevant to the conditions brought about by the pandemic.

## Transformational Leadership and Leadership as a Practice

Amongst these leadership theories are transformational leadership and leadership by practice which depart from the focus on individual leader's traits, behaviours, and norms towards a more fundamentally relational and morally reflective, interactive and communicative relationship between a leader and their followers. Transformational leadership and leadership as a practice are highly reflective in their nature and aim to focus on influencing others to achieve a positive impact on both the participants and their organisations. Transformational leadership inherently reflects and addresses potential marginalisation and strives to enhance the participatory management and practice by empowering others (Frank, 2002).

## Collective and Shared Leadership

Transformational leadership and leadership by practice intersect profoundly with collective and shared leadership theories. These theories conceptualise leadership as a multi-directional exchange of power influence, that stretches beyond an organisation, to create a positive change in society through a *dialogic process* promoting collective learning. This shared leadership focuses on a dialogical process empowering people to engage in a deeper level of participation. Collective and shared leadership theories also endorse the role of followers as active social influencers over their leaders (Oc & Bashshur, 2013).

## Deliberative Leadership

Similarly, deliberative leadership is the engagement of followers in a deliberative and consultative decision-making process, by the dispersion of power by leaders, to achieve peacebuilding goals (Lees-Marshment, 2015). Deliberative leadership acknowledges that leaders cannot achieve goals on their own and therefore relies on diverse followers' input and feedback (ibid.). This is fundamental for peacebuilding CSOs as leaders play a big role in the decision-making process of the improvement of their communities' lives. Further, the emphasis on inclusion and meaningful deliberation in the decision-making process, instead of the use of power and coercion, not only increases the legitimacy of decisions but also results in more buy-in from the community and addresses issues of unjust power structures (Kuyper, 2012).

## Place-based Leadership

Similar to transformational, collective and shared leadership theories, place-based leadership acknowledges the role of followers in leadership since it explicitly defines roles of collaboration in a networked setting to achieve social outcomes. Place-based leadership can be defined as the process of improving the quality of life for communities and advancing social justice in a particular place (Hambleton, 2014). Placed-based leadership, thus, adopts a more dynamic understanding of leadership and recognises the importance of local and informal networks to advance the transformation of social spaces, such as peacebuilding.

## Pluralistic and Participatory Leadership

Deliberative leadership and non-coercive decision-making require power-sharing and inclusion. Pluralistic and participatory leadership relies on the inclusion of members of the community in the design and implementation of peacebuilding initiatives. Participatory and pluralistic leadership is consultative in nature, creating and disseminating knowledge amongst leaders and followers to reach evidence-based decisions (Kuyper, 2012). Moreover, pluralistic leadership acknowledges leaders' power that influences accountability and reciprocity and acts toward the inclusion of those affected by conflict in the decision-making process for peacebuilding (Kezar, 2000a, 2000b). Furthermore, it is argued that a leader's positionality such as their gender, race, and role, can affect the interpretation of leadership by followers which could result in biases (Cox, 1994; Kezar, 2000a, 2000b). The multi-dimensionality of pluralistic leadership inherently promotes diversity and inclusion minimising biases and intergroup conflict (ibid.).

## Transformational, Collective, Place-based, Deliberative, and Pluralistic and Participatory Leadership

This chapter, therefore, conceptualises a hybrid understanding of leadership in the civil society sphere, referred to as hybrid leadership hereafter, as the intersection of leadership as collective and shared, transformational, pluralistic and participatory, deliberative, and place-based. This hybrid leadership departs from the traditional narrative of merely personal traits and roles expected from individuals and an inherent unequal distribution of power and influence between leaders and followers, towards a more dynamic social process. This leadership is more reflective, dialogical, deliberative, promotes diversity and deeper levels of participation, and adopts a multi-directional exchange of power and influence between leaders and followers by nature. In contrast, traditional leadership is simplistic and hierarchal, which often leads to the centralisation of power impeding efforts for increased participation.

## Recommendations

Accordingly, this *hybrid leadership* acknowledges the role of engaged citizens or followers in creating positive democratic social change at different levels, including the local level, and influencing leaders through the collaboration of various stakeholders in a networked setting. This networked setting induces inclusive dialogue and deliberation between conflict parties, providing the conditions that contribute to long-lasting and effective peacebuilding (Oc & Bashshur, 2013). This leadership also underscores the importance of dialogic processes to achieve social good, which translates to more effective peacebuilding.

Furthermore, leadership that relies on a multi-directional exchange of power also minimises leadership bias amongst peacebuilding leaders and followers, promotes a reflective and reflexive practice, and improves feedback mechanisms contributing to more inclusive and effective OPDs. This practice can address issues of leadership coercion and unjust and imbalanced power structures that can lead to the potential marginalisation of some groups, especially in complex and nascent platforms such as Clubhouse (Kemmis & McTaggart, 2005; Kuyper, 2012).

Further, deliberative leadership is thought to improve relations between leaders and followers, especially for traditional and grassroots communities who are typically overlooked in peacebuilding activities. This hybrid leadership theory, which gives power to followers, synchronises with participatory methodologies as it involves those affected by the problem, such as local and marginalised groups, in the design, implementation, and monitoring of their peacebuilding projects. This offers opportunities for enhanced linkages between different tracks of peace talks and the effective participation and leadership of women as peacebuilders in peacebuilding which is instrumental for longer-lasting conflict resolution. However, participants confirmed that the inclusion of marginalised groups on its own does not guarantee conducive peace and CSO leadership should induce meaningful deliberation in a safe space that allows free and open dialogue (Kuyper, 2012).

Moreover, this focus on grassroots and locally led initiatives should result in more relevant and effective peacebuilding initiatives and improve the understanding of peacebuilding best practices, since they are best harnessed by the knowledge of local actors and leaders. Further, the adoption of pluralistic and participatory leadership theories is even more imperative in conflict settings since peacebuilding relies on the meaningful participation, activism, and engagement of local stakeholders who are more cognisant of local conflict dynamics and reconciliation needs (Saleeby et al., 2014; Autesserre & Alexander, 2021). In contrast, traditional peacebuilding approaches rely on foreign-led peacebuilders who may lack the in-depth understanding of local societies and cultures, potentially resulting in less encapsulation of the true drivers of conflict (Autesserre & Alexander, 2021).

Engaging participants in deliberative and collaborative peacebuilding activities in a safe space and with a common goal can add ownership to peacebuilding processes and reduce intergroup tensions, divisions, and prejudices, promoting long-lasting reconciliation (Hirschmann & Doesum, 2021; Autesserre & Alexander, 2021). Furthermore, evidence shows that participatory and deliberative mechanisms, especially when accompanied by online tools, can strengthen community mobilisation and learning, improving local capacities to identify and tackle local challenges (IIED, 2020).

To address issues of elite domination over OPD and respond to calls by marginalised groups to represent themselves, CSO leaders should accommodate participants without internet access by adopting a 'blended approach' that complements OPD with an offline and face-to-face component whenever possible (Hernandez & Roberts, 2018; Kassoumeh, 2020). CSO leaders should also improve access to technology for under-resourced, under-represented, and remote and poorly connected communities (Peace Direct, 2020). In all contexts covered by this study, CSO leaders are providing internet access and covering internet costs to ensure marginalised groups are able to join these dialogues. In remote areas in Yemen, community centres are equipped with internet and laptops so locals can join discussions as a group, instead of separately. Leaders are also training locals on the use of technology and providing community leaders with digital tools. In Syria, CSO leaders are requesting the provision of Virtual Private Network (VPN) subscriptions to participants to bypass government surveillance (Anonymous, 2020).

To improve dialogue facilitation skills and overcome potential issues of unbalanced participation, leaders should undergo training on inclusion and effective dialogue that relies on sharing, listening, and inquiring (Escobar et al., 2014). This is crucial as dialogue facilitation is amongst the biggest challenges for leaders, especially when moderating complicated and nascent spaces like Clubhouse discussions. This should also inherently reduce 'Zoom Fatigue,' which is becoming increasingly prevalent in OPDs.

Furthermore, to overcome issues of INGOs' absence on the ground, INGOs should also adopt the hybrid leadership which pushes the localisation and systems change agenda and empowers local CSOs improving accountability and oversight through collaboration and transformation. This empowerment would give local CSOs the freedom to identify problems, propose solutions, and determine outcomes and goals that are more locally contextualised and inclusive reducing ethnic, political, and other biases (Cole, 2012). This focus on sub-national peacebuilding brought about by the use of hybrid leadership creates added opportunities for an increased sense of belonging, ownership, and positive connection leading to sustainable peace through a dialogic change process (Agger-Gupta & Harris, 2017).

## Conclusion

This chapter contributes both normatively and empirically to a better understanding of the challenges and opportunities faced by peacebuilding CSO leaders when using online tools to conduct peacebuilding dialogue during the Covid-19 pandemic and beyond.

While the reliance on online tools to conduct virtual peacebuilding dialogue has offered opportunities for a wider inclusion of various previously marginalised groups, the use of technology has also amplified the marginalisation of other groups who lack the knowledge and accessibility to such technologies. These groups are in most cases those who are affected by conflict which risks the dismissal of the root causes of conflict and potentially results in the magnification of grievances, fuelling conflict or contributing to unsustainable peace. Furthermore, the use of complex and nascent online spaces, such as Clubhouse, which is mostly used by the youth and available solely by invitation and to iPhone users, reinforces inequalities and elite capture, further marginalising certain groups.

The pandemic has offered an invaluable opportunity to reflect on the peacebuilding sector, practice, and theory, offering lessons and recommendations beyond the pandemic. For example, respondents underscored that although the absence of INGOs has pushed the localisation and systems change agendas giving more autonomy and power to local initiatives to design and implement their own peacebuilding projects, there are adverse effects on peacebuilding as INGO roles of oversight and accountability are deteriorated. Research participants highlighted leadership selection biases when inviting dialogue participants, further impeding the efficiency of peacebuilding dialogue.

To minimise these issues, this chapter presents prospects for improving the peacebuilding practice by recommending that CSO leaders adopt a transformational, collective, place-based, deliberative, and pluralistic and participatory leadership, which is reflective in practice and promotes higher levels of meaningful participation and inclusion. Additionally, this leadership acknowledges the true power of followers, addresses power imbalances, promotes collective learning, and reduces biases in contrast to traditional leadership, which is often hierarchical and focuses on personal traits. Participatory, collective, pluralistic, and deliberative leadership aims to engage conflict-affected groups in collaborative and deliberative peacebuilding activities which can address the root causes of conflict, contributing to conducive peace. Deliberative and participatory leadership involves those affected by conflict in the design and implementation of peacebuilding projects resulting in more buy-in. Place-based leadership also highlights the importance of informal networks to improve social spaces which could be beneficial for peacebuilding work. CSO leaders should improve their online dialogue facilitation skills to ensure they are inclusive, effective, and rely on sharing, listening, and inquiring.

Similarly, international organisations should also adopt this hybrid leadership that empowers locally led peacebuilding initiatives and promotes participatory design and implementation of peacebuilding projects, which are more contextually relevant and promote higher upward accountability and oversight given their absence on the ground due to travel restrictions.

Finally, further research is required to explore the utilisation of drop-in audio chat apps, such as Clubhouse, to conduct peacebuilding dialogue as this space remains unexplored.

## References

Agger-Gupta, N., & Harris, B. (2017). Dialogic change and the practice of inclusive leadership. In A. Moras, R. Dutra, & H. Schochman (Eds.), *Breaking the zero-sum game (building leadership bridges)* (pp. 305–322). Emerald Publishing Limited.

Aladwar, S. (2021). [Interview] (08 05 2021).

Alberti, C. and Clark, S. (2020). The challenge of peacebuilding during a pandemic. LSE Covid 19 Blog (21 October 2020). Accessed January 19, 2022 http://eprints.lse.ac.uk/107271/1/covid19_2020_10_21_the_challenge_of_peacebuilding_during_a.pdf

Anonymous. (2020). [Interview] (18 08 2020).

Autesserre, S., & Alexander, J. (2021). *Building peace, from the bottom up: A Q&A with Séverine Autesserre* [Online]. Accessed May 24, 2021. https://www.thenewhumanitarian.org/interview/2021/5/13/building-peace-from-the-bottom-up-severine-autesserre.

Bangkok Post. (2021). *Controversy amid camaraderie* [Online]. https://www.bangkokpost.com/life/social-and-lifestyle/2077379/controversy-amid-camaraderie.

Beaton, B., Perley, D., George, C., & O'Donnell, S. (2017). Engaging remote marginalized communities using appropriate online research methods. In N. Fielding, R. Lee, & G. Blank (Eds.), *The SAGE handbook of online research methods* (pp. 563–577). SAGE Publications Ltd.

Bell, C., Epple, T., & Pospisil, J. (2020). *The impact of covid-19 on peace and transition processes: Tracking the trends*. Political Settlements Research Programme (PSRP).

Bickmore, K. (2014). Peacebuilding dialogue pedagogies in Canadian classrooms. *Curriculum Inquiry, 44*(4), 553–582.

Cole, M. J. (2012). *Investigating the inclusion of ethno-depoliticization within peace-building policies in postconflict Sierra Leone*. University of Ottawa.

Conducive Space for Peace. (2020). *New report: Act now on 'localisation': COVID-19 implications for funding to local peacebuilding*. Conducive Space for Peace.

Conducive Space for Peace. (2021). *THE DRAGONFLY MODEL systems change to strengthen support for locally-led peacebuilding*. Conducive Space for Peace.

Cornwall, A., & Jewkes, R. (1995). What is participatory research? *Social Science & Medicine, 41*(12), 1667–1676.

Cox, T. (1994). *Cultural diversity in organizations: Theory, research and practice*. Berrett-Koehler Publishers.

Edes, B., & Garrison, J. (2021). *COVID-19 has boosted civil society participation in international meetings despite technical glitches* [Online]. https://www.orfonline.org/expert-speak/covid-19-has-boosted-civil-society-participation-in-international-meetings-despite-technical-glitches/

Escobar, O., Faulkner, W., & Rea, H. J. (2014). Building capacity for dialogue facilitation in public engagement. *Journal of Dialogue Studies, 2*(1), 87–111.

Frank, J. W. (2002). *Transformational leadership and moral discourse in the workplace and civil society* [Online]. https://digitalcommons.unf.edu/etd/212

Fredendall, L. D., Robbins, T., & Moore, D. (2001). The influence of instructor leadership on student commitment and performance. *Educational Research Quarterly, 24*(4), 55.

FriEnt. (2021). *Twitter* [Online]. https://twitter.com/FriEnt_news/status/1389961498450083846.

Guzman, M., Kadima, C., Lovell, G., Mohamed, A. A., Norton, R., Rivas, F., & Thiam, A. (2016). Making connections in the 'White-walled labyrinth'. In *People's knowledge and participatory action research* (pp. 23–32). Practical Action Publishing Ltd.

Hambleton, R. (2014). Place-based innovation for a bounded planet. Policy press scholarship online. https://policypress.universitypressscholarship.com/view/10.1332/policypress/9781447304975.001.0001/upso-9781447304975-chapter-5

Helmi, K. (2021). [Interview] (05 05 2021).

Hernandez, K., & Roberts, T. (2018). *Leaving no one behind in a digital world. K4D emerging issues report*. Brighton, UK: Institute of Development Studies, 1–24.

Hirschmann, G. K., & Doesum, N. J. V. (2021). Playing with the enemy Investigating the impact of musical peacebuilding. *Peace and Conflict Journal of Peace Psychology*, 2–15.

IIED. (2020). *Informal settlement data and local community responses to COVID-19 and climate risks* [Online]. https://www.iied.org/informal-settlement-data-local-community-responses-covid-19-climate-risks.

International Alert. (2020). *Can we build peace from a distance? The impact of COVID-19 on the peacebuilding sector*. International Alert.

Kassoumeh, B. (2020). Online peace-building dialogue: Opportunities & challenges post-covid-19 pandemic emergence. *Journal of Dialogue Studies*, 87–105.

Kemmis, S., & McTaggart, R. (2005). Participatory action research: Communicative action and the public sphere. In N. K. Denzin & Y. S. Lincoln (Eds.), *The Sage handbook of qualitative research* (pp. 559–603). Sage Publications Ltd.

Kezar, A. (2000a). Pluralistic leadership. *The Journal of Higher Education*, 71(6), 722–743.

Kezar, A. (2000b). Pluralistic leadership: Bringing diverse voices to the table. *About Campus*, 5(3), 6–11.

Kuyper J., (2012). Deliberative democracy and the neglected dimension of leadership. *Journal of Public Deliberation*, 8(1), 1–26. https://doi.org/10.16997/jdd.126

Lees-Marshment, J. (2015). *The ministry of public input: Integrating citizen views into political leadership*. Palgrave Macmillan, 220–247.

Leonardsson, H., & Rudd, G. (2015). The 'local turn' in peacebuilding: A literature review of effective and emancipatory local peacebuilding. *Third World Quarterly*, 36(5), 825–839.

Mac Observer. (2021). *Clubhouse is one of the most popular apps in the world – But what is it?* [Online]. https://www.macobserver.com/news/clubhouse-is-one-of-the-most-popular-apps-in-the-world-but-what-is-it/.

Mansour, N. (2021). [Interview] (03 05 2021).

Mashhour, H. (2021). [Interview] (02 05 2021).

Mckay, S. (2011). *Participatory action research, community-based. The encyclopedia of peace psychology*. Wiley Online library. https://doi.org/10.1002/9780470672532.wbepp186

Oc, B., & Bashshur, M. R. (2013). Followership, leadership and social influence. *Leadership Quarterly*, 24(6), 919–934.

Peace Direct. (2020). *Digital pathways for peace insights and lessons from a global online consultation*. Peace Direct.

Saleeby, E., Holschneider, C. H., & Singhal, R. (2014). Paradigm shifts: Using a participatory leadership process to redesign health systems. *Current Opinion in Obstetrics & Gynecology*, 26(6), 516–522.

# 5 Common Minimum Universe
## Role of Youth Leadership in Community Development

*Vijayendra Kadalabal, Swathi Pottabathini, Kumar Gaurav*

## Introduction

Social networks can be seen as basic building blocks of societies that enable social interaction and cohesion. Though there have been varying definitions and assorted relational words, in simple terms, a social network is a 'structure of relationships linking social actors' (Marsden, cited in Pescosolido, 2011) or 'the set of actors and the ties among them' (Wasserman & Faust, 1994, cited in Pescosolido, 2011).

Social networks have been an innate component of even the ancient societies with flourishing inter-regional and intra-regional trade and travel since the Harappan and Mesopotamian civilizations. But these were 'parochial' (Suchman 1964, Pescosolido, 2011) in the sense that they were encompassing and provided solidarity to the in-groups but were often intolerant of the out-groups (Blau and Giddens, cited in Pescosolido, 2011). As technological advancements furthered with the advent of the 'Renaissance' and 'Enlightenment,' these networks were strengthened and widened with the spread of religion, wars, colonisation, and industrialisation. The resulting modernity was accompanied by the buzzword – globalisation. Sociologists Martin Albrow and Elizabeth King define it as 'all those processes by which the peoples of the world are incorporated into a single world society.' This 'single world society' can be viewed as an interconnected network of social networks that further not only stimulated the 'digital revolution' but also was itself perpetuated as its consequence. These social networks are more tolerant of the out-groups that help their widening, but the members deal with a lack of solidarity stemming from uncertainty (Pescosolido, 2011).

Communication has been a conduit that connects social networks, both internally and externally. Over time, globalisation has strengthened the process with the massive use of technology that forms the basis of modern social networking sites and mass media. Manuel Castells, in his seminal

DOI: 10.4324/9781003288145-5

work, *The Rise of Network Society*, calls the society that is characterised by globalisation and ICT as a 'network society':

> A society whose social structure is made up of networks powered by micro-electronics-based information and communications technologies.

This *network society* has been able to leverage various social groups to work towards the common goal of building a better world through campaigns, petitions, awareness generation, etc. One of the most important of such social groups being the youth. The word youth has always been perceived as a synonym of energy and change, where the story is fresh to be told to the world. The idea of the word 'youth' is related to the physical age of the person, but it's not merely biological, it's also a social construct that is shaped by the society and which in turn shapes the society. The United Nations, for statistical purposes, defines 'youth' as those persons between the ages of 15 and 24 years. The Secretary General recognised that, apart from that statistical definition, the meaning of the term 'youth' varies in different societies around the world (UN, 2020). As per India's Census 2011, Youth (15 to 24 years) in India constitutes one-fifth (19.1%) of India's total population – a significant percentage that is a potential reservoir for bringing social change and development (GOI, 2017).

Today's youth, consisting of Generation Z and Generation Alpha, are unique due to their extensive exposure to technology even before their birth. Their communication has largely been shaped by globalisation, from the use of social networking sites like Facebook, WhatsApp, and LinkedIn, microblogging sites like Twitter, media sharing sites like YouTube, to news and discussion sites like Quora. The content could be generated in one corner of the world and yet accessible for consumption in another. This has created 'imagined communities' (Anderson, 2006) that comprise of members panning across social identities and geographical boundaries.

## Covid-19 and the World

According to the World Health Organisation (WHO), 'Coronavirus disease (Covid-19) is an infectious disease caused by a newly discovered coronavirus.' Coronaviruses are a large family of viruses that have existed before and have been the cause of minor illnesses like the common cold to severe ones like Middle East Respiratory Syndrome (MERS) and Severe Acute Respiratory Syndrome (SARS). What sets apart the novel coronavirus that causes Covid-19 is that it is a new strain of coronavirus that has not been previously identified in humans (WHO, 2020). This means a vaccine is yet to be invented and, in the meanwhile, the disease has been spreading like wildfire with high transmissibility and binding affinity of the virus (Kumar et al., 2020).

With its origin in China and later spread to Europe, followed by the US and India, and its current expansion to more than 180 countries, it emerged as a pandemic of gigantic proportions, never heard of in recent times. This has led to nations formulating immediate protocols and policies to protect their citizens including physical distancing, wearing masks, using sanitizers, and announcing nationwide lockdowns to curtail mass movement and contact.

On 30 January 2020, Covid-19 was declared as a Public Health Emergency of International Concern by the World Health Organisation and it was on this very day that India reported its first case in the state of Kerala (Kumar et al., 2020). Subsequently, the drastic rise in cases led to the imposition of 'Janata Curfew' and later one of the strictest lockdowns of the world in India. As of 21 August 2020, India witnessed a total of 2,905,823 cases and a death toll of 54,849 (India, 2020).

Covid-19 has had severe implications on various communities, especially the marginalised sections and the frontline workers including the medical fraternity and administration personnel. Women have been one such segment that has been at the forefront of bearing the unequal consequences with reports of a twofold rise in complaints of domestic violence, an increased share of the household burden, and a higher risk of losing jobs (Beniwal, 2020). Further, children have become vulnerable at various levels such as an increase in poverty, violence/abuse, loss, or fear of loss of loved ones, and disruption of education/peer activities leading to mental health issues such as anxiety (Kumar et al., 2020).

For this chapter, we will limit ourselves to a detailed study of the impact on two communities, namely migrants and youth, and how leadership emerged within them.

**Migrants:** Internal migrants in India comprise primarily seasonal/temporary workers who shift from rural to urban areas in search of work that is usually unskilled, low paid, informal, and without any social security (Zeitlyn et al., 2014). These migrants are nearly 100 million in number, constituting a reasonable chunk of the Indian economy, based on an official employment estimation (Deshingkar & Akter, 2009). Despite being the drivers of the Indian economy, they were left to fend for themselves during the lockdown. Millions of them walked on foot, rode bicycles, and gave up large portions of their hard-earned savings on transport to leave the cities that had abandoned them, to respond to the 'ritual tug of home' in villages. Covid-19 has entrenched their deprivations further such as poverty, malnutrition, lack of access to healthcare, poor/crowded living conditions and such, due to heightened vulnerability to the disease, massive economic slowdown causing job losses, and psychological consequences of such multiple stresses due to the aforementioned deprivations (Ranjana, 2020).

**Youth:** The Indian economy was facing a twin crisis even in the pre-Covid-19 times with high unemployment of 6.1% and the highest education loan NPAs (Non-Performing Assets) in banks, proving to be the Achilles' heel to the maximum utilisation of demographic dividend (Pettiwala, 2020). Covid-19 has only worsened the situation with one report jointly published by the International Labour Organisation (ILO) and the Asian Development Bank (ADB) suggesting that nearly 41% lakh youth in the country lost jobs due to the pandemic, of which farm and construction workers account for the highest number (TOI, 2020).

Considering India's demographic dividend, more than 60% of the population lying in the age group of 15 to 29, his words ring true even today. The total youth population increased in India from 168 million in 1971 to 423 million in 2011. The share of the youth population in the total population has been increasing continuously from the level of 30.6% in the year 1971 to 34.8% in the year 2011. However, the increase in the number of youths in India also has a different dynamic, when looked at from the angle of community development. If we bring in a few facts to determine the social status of youth in terms of education and employment share in India, a different picture emerges (GOI, 2017).

In India as per the census of 2011 (Census, 2011), the total illiteracy percentage was 39% which when gender-segregated, translates to 21% in male and 41% in females (Age-15 & Above, Census-2011). The overall unemployment rate peaked at 23.5% during the Covid-19 pandemic (Trading Economics, 2020), i.e., nearly tripled from the pre-Covid-19 times.

Further, on the education front with the closure of educational institutions, though there has been a shift towards online learning – it has proven to be discriminatory. A digital divide exists in India, especially in the rural areas where according to the Key Indicators of Household Social Consumption on Education in India report, based on the 2017–18 National Sample Survey, less than 15% of rural Indian households have the internet as opposed to 42% urban Indian households (Sudevan, 2020). This has led to several disruptions to learning and even suicides among students who couldn't cope with the challenges of online learning. Further, for the disabled students, without the necessary support in terms of technology and social guidance, the situation proves extremely challenging. In addition to this, the youth are exposed to mental illnesses such as depression and anxiety with ILO reporting 50% of global youth reporting it (Business Standard, 2020), due to staying indoors and without sufficient physical and mental activities, excessive media usage, a looming risk of a disease, and an unpromising future.

**Leadership:** Leadership is a ubiquitous word, yet there is no one single definition of it – to each their own. For this paper, we would use the following as the operational definition of leadership and see if there is a possibility of tying the two strands of youth and migrants with it.

> Leadership is about mobilizing people, predicting future directions, leading your team towards success, caring about people who work with you and who depend on your services. But this alone does not define a leader. Leadership is also about styles and skills, and about using the right styles and skills in the right place at the right time.
>
> (Kumaran, 2012)

Leadership is thus a perfect blend of vision and character, in addition to skills and activities. It involves doing difficult things, and this can be done only through commitment and dedication that stems from the underlying foundation of trust among the team members. A leader is looked at as the ethical and moral compass by the team and they have to stick to it even in times of crisis (Lexa, 2017). Though great leaders usually anticipate and eliminate the occurrence of crises, they do have to face some unavoidable ones. In these times, their trademark lies in spearheading meticulous planning and execution on the ground, in addition to being self-involved with the team. Further, leadership doesn't stop with the ending of a crisis but creates new learnings and opportunities to better tackle future challenges (Lexa, 2017).

## The Public Health Crisis and India

When the pandemic reached India, as preventive mitigation measures, India initiated harsh controls, asking 1.3 billion people to stay at home for the period of lockdown with few urgent exceptions resulted in countrywide lockdown imposed for several months, which resulted in migrant exodus (Sengupta & Jha, 2020). The public health crisis thus becomes a humanitarian crisis. The panic arose because of the pandemic and imposition of strict lockdown, the workers started walking towards bus stops, railway stations, and unable to find the options available to travel to their distant rural homes, a few even started walking towards their home.

The point of the lockdown measure was to initiate 'social distancing' to prevent the spread of infection. But there was no way that the migrant workers could fulfil those conditions in their temporary, cramped urban homes without work, income, or social protection (Sengupta & Jha, 2020). However, this arises because of the loss of confidence in the Indian medical delivery system. India has an unequal medical delivery system. While the rich Indians can get good health services in private hospitals and clinics, villages in rural India are bereft of any public health services. Areas of urban poverty are also similarly deprived. The Indian government takes care of only 27% of health expenditure, spending only 1% of GDP on health. India is one of the countries with the lowest public health spending (Tiwari, 2020).

When the migrant exodus took place, the dynamic component of migration exacerbated the epidemic in the country, with several studies showing that migration led to a spread of the pandemic. There are also studies suggesting that it's also vice versa, migration leads to the spread of infection and the pandemic affecting migration and migrants (Sengupta & Jha, 2020).

## The Migrant Exodus

In India, migrants constitute 38% of the total population (Census, 2011). This got worse when the pandemic arrived in India which resulted in a lockdown that began in March 2020. The lockdown has severely impacted migrants, several lost their jobs and got stranded outside their native places, fear of infection and uncertainty of the recent development forced them to move towards their home. When they did not find the transport to go back to their homes, many of them started walking, and some completed the journey of more than thousands of kilometres.

Many died while walking, including the incident of migrants run over by the train. Those who weren't able to travel back faced acute hunger mainly because the impact of the lockdown hit in two ways: first shortage of food and second unavailability of money to buy food (Biswas, 2020). These impacts troubled the low-income households, which were less well positioned to cope with earnings losses with no alternative source of earnings and social security coverage. Migrant workers constitute quite a large proportion of such vulnerable populations, which also get multiplied because of social factors of marginalisation (Khanna, 2020).

## Voices Unheard: A Case Study of Covid-19 Relief in India

A group of young volunteers in India got together to form a strong informal network of individuals which assisted more than 30,000 individuals during the pandemic-infused lockdowns in India. While the core group of volunteers engaged primarily through telephonic conversations, the fact that for three months they were able to continuously facilitate resources (both financial and non-financial) is a case in itself.

The unique system which relied on trust, transparency, and empathy ensured that any individual who contributed received details of the beneficiaries along with the photographs and contact details (if they wished to speak to them). The relief had two phases – first, which was more of a personal fundraiser, through an appeal sent out to friends and families, and second, set up through a fundraiser portal, Milaap, gave the team the opportunity to leverage their international networks.

In this chapter, we are interested in exploring the various factors which made this relief possible.

## Research Objective

The objective of this study is to understand:

1. How did the Covid/lockdown affect individuals?
2. What role did the social network sites play in this relief exercise?
3. Did leadership play a role in carrying out the relief?

## Methodology

The sample is purposive and consists of three groups of respondents: The Beneficiaries, The Donors, and the Volunteers. The donor and the volunteer answered the same questionnaire and the beneficiaries responded to the set of questions over a phone call. The research tool is a Semi-Structured Interview which was designed with a common theme for all the three groups of respondents but customised keeping in mind the difference in engagements.

## Findings

The group of respondents involving donors and volunteers was a little complicated as many of them had also offered their assistance as volunteers. Therefore, we allowed the respondents to identify themselves as a donor or a volunteer or both. Eight respondents clearly identified themselves as donor, three respondents as volunteer and one of the respondents identified themselves as both donor/volunteers. In all, 12 respondents were interviewed in this section through a Google form (that all of them could access and use).

In the case of beneficiaries, phone calls were made, and their responses were transcribed simultaneously as this group of respondents had their limitations with respect to accessing or filling a Google form. All of our respondents are kept anonymous for the sake of their privacy.

## Impact of Covid-19 and the Resulting Lockdown

The direct impact of the pandemic, as well as the lockdown, was different for the beneficiary group and very different for the donor/volunteer group. The beneficiary group expressed their experience of Covid-19 through issues of Hunger, Livelihood, and Police Brutality in addition to the fear of the pandemic.

> We were literally starving, we get our payments on a daily basis, after lockdown, the company has given some amount but that did not last, since the government extended lockdown. We have several families here who have children, we can manage few days without food, but they cannot survive. we were planning to walk to our home town in Bihar, which is around 1500 km.
>
> – *One of many beneficiaries*

The donor/volunteer group did not experience any direct loss of livelihood. Even though this group experienced helplessness, it was more to do with what was happening around them rather than what was happening with them. The donor/volunteer group also acknowledged their privilege and kept themselves engaged in hope reinforcing activities.

> Covid and the subsequent lockdowns have hit all irrespectively. However, the most hit were those who were dependent highly on monthly salaries more so for those dependent on daily wages/income. Having read this news and watching the plight of so many around and not being able to support was overwhelming. Having seen the goodness of people around to support me when I was suffering due to a sickness made my faith in goodness more. I wanted to give back to society. Watching the news of migrants walking long miles, kids crying of tiredness and hunger while walking back with their families to their villages was heart-wrenching
>
> -*One of the donors*

It can be clearly seen that people who were dependent on daily wages for survival were more directly impacted due to the lockdown.

Also, when asked about what alternatives were available to the beneficiary groups, the common answer was twofold – returning home (since they were migrants) or total absence of any other alternative. This also highlights the importance of this relief work in reaching those who couldn't be reached. The fact that this was possible with very minimal field presence and the relief that took place across the country is also worth noting.

> There was no strategy, we have nowhere to go since when you go out police will beat you. It was all up to the almighty God to help us
> *-Beneficiary*

## Social Media and the Relief

As mentioned earlier, the relief team was coordinating remotely from different parts of the country. Hence, the role of social media in both facilitating and reaching for help needs to be highlighted. The respondents from all these groups reinforced our assumption here. It was found that WhatsApp, Facebook, and Instagram played a significant role in spreading the message during the relief – mainly for the search for donors/volunteers and also the personal networks the relief team was using.

> I was approached by Rajiv (names changed) to see if I would want to support a group of migrants stuck with no food and supplies in Ludhiana, Punjab. That time I was able to offer financial assistance to the group. Since Gaurav was handling the case then, I was also in touch with him. After the group was able to get support with the help of my contribution, Gaurav gave me the number of a migrant laborer Pramod from that group to check the progress. I ended up calling Pramod. Pramod was so happy and thankful for the support and the voice of relief was so peaceful to my ears. During that call, Pramod also asked for additional help for another group of 30 people stuck somewhere near to his place. On hearing this, I felt it to be my responsibility to help them. I reached out to Gaurav to see what can be done. And one thing led to another, and before I knew it, I was physically, mentally, and emotionally involved in the process
> *Donor/Volunteer*

While with the beneficiary group, it was more of word of mouth through a mobile phone or WhatsApp forwards which led them to contact the relief team. In both cases, the role of personal networks and the willingness to assist those in need needs to be highlighted.

> I came to know about your team from a friend in Bihar, who told us that these people are helping those who are in distress because of lockdown. I got your WhatsApp number, where I sent you the details of the person in distress
>
> *-Beneficiary*

## Transparency and Snowballing

There are networks each of us built before the evolution of the social networks as such. This case study is a classic example of how social networks as well as the traditional networks came together to make things happen for the communities and individuals involved.

Most of the respondents in the donor group identified that since they got details about how their initial contribution was utilised, they were confident in the relief work reaching people and spreading the word amongst their own networks. Therefore, the transparency which was adopted resulted in a snowballing effect with respect to the donors' group.

When asked if they received details about the usage of funds and how they felt about it, these were some of the responses from the donors.

> Oh yes. I am still in touch with one of them who says I am like an elder sister to her. And it gives more meaning to my existence as a human
>
> Since during these times there were many people who were working on relief work, it was difficult to differentiate between the genuine and otherwise. What worked best for this group is the word of mouth through credible sources: I initially supported because I trusted Rajiv (name changed), people from my network gave financial support because they trusted me, some social media influencers also joined our efforts because they heard about it from their trusted sources and so on

While transparency helped, it was interesting to know that the beneficiary group did not find the donors contacting them as a breach of privacy in any way. Rather they very much appreciated that they got to speak to the people who helped them. The crisis in a way brought unknown communities together under the umbrella of relief.

When the beneficiaries were asked, if any of the donors contacted them and how they felt about it, these were some of their responses.

> Yes, all the time. I came to know that I was helped by a South Indian man, I was very delighted as I have never spoken to a person from South India before. I was thinking, why did he help me?

Yes, a large group of people have together discussed with me. I was feeling so motivated, it was one of the special moments in my life

Yes, after every help, it felt so good. People who don't know us are helping from other parts of the country, we have not met before, but we received help from them. Hope someday will try to meet them

Even in the case of the beneficiaries, it was clear that they did not shy away from reaching out to their friends who needed assistance. When asked if they thought of connecting the relief team to other communities like themselves, affected by the pandemic, their response was affirmative.

I have been a single point of contact for 50-plus families in Ludhiana, the information that your team is helping people in distress has also given them hope. I collected all the information required, and sent it to your team on WhatsApp, have also made videos and taken photographs for the authenticity of the case. It would have been very selfish if you would not have reacted to their appeal

## Nature of the Relief

The fact that this was a voluntary youth group operating on the strength of their social capital across the nation (for relief) and beyond (for fundraising) meant that the group was able to mobilise resources to critical areas irrespective of geography.

It can be seen clearly that the majority of the support was provided by linking the needy to partner organisations. The outreach of this kind might have not been possible had the youth group been part of an organisation that would more often than not have a localised presence due to geographical limitations.

## Limitations

The authors acknowledge that due to paucity of time and circumstances, the sample size could not be larger. This forms one of the major limitations of this study. Besides, the fact that the authors were themselves involved in the core relief work brings in an inherent bias to the study. However, the research was designed keeping in mind the above facts, and an attempt to minimise the bias, if any, was made.

## Conclusion

Young India is responsive and adept with new forms of networking bringing out leaders within them quite naturally. This is something this case study reinforces, considering that most participants in the relief group, donor group as well as volunteer group were youth and showed leadership either by mobilising resources, amplifying the message, or aggregating efforts.

With the communities at the heart of it, the local networks in terms of organisations working in the sector or reaching the needy communities were adeptly utilised. At the same time, the fundraiser was able to mobilise some funds inclusive of global networks (outside India). This highlights the local to global outreach adopted.

The beneficiary group as well as the donor/volunteer group acknowledged the plight of the communities which faced the immediate brunt of the lockdown. The respondents showed keen interest in ensuring the social well-being of the individuals/communities which were in the middle of the crisis. This can be referred to as the 'Common Minimal Universe' which we all aspire for and forms the major driving force to enable communities to survive in crises. In terms of how one can look at the operational part of the relief, the process can be divided into three phases: Aggregation, Resource Mobilisation, and Amplification.

- **Aggregation**: This refers to the coming together of the volunteer youth group, the different organisations which partnered with them, the communities which reached out to them, or any other aspect which aggregated the impact of the relief and made it a large-scale community affair rather than an individual effort.
- **Resource Mobilisation**: This refers to the ways and means of mobilising fundraising-related resources through social media and the mobilisation of volunteers on the ground when required. No kind of relief would have reached the impacted communities if not for the volunteers.
- **Amplification**: This refers to the scale of the resources mobilised and the role of social media in amplifying them. Be it word-of-mouth publicity resorted to by the beneficiaries or the social media forwards which attracted more donors and volunteers, the scale was made possible due to the amplification.
- **Leadership**: Any individual who showed any of these attributes either in singular form or a combination of two or more is considered as a leader in our case study, thereby making leadership the enabling factor for the relief to take place on the ground at such a scale.

The three processes aggregation, resource mobilisation, and amplification came together enabled by the leadership of young individuals in various social groups involved to ensure the common minimum universe which every group involved in the relief (beneficiary, donor, volunteer) aspired for – social well-being.

# References

Anderson, B. (2006). *Imagined communities: Reflections on the origin and spread of nationalism*. Verso Books.

Beniwal, V. (2020). *NDTV* [Online]. Accessed June 27, 2020. https://www.ndtv.com/india-news/coronavirus-impact-worsens-gender-gap-indias-painful-shecession-2253037.

Biswas, S. (2020). *BBC* [Online]. Accessed May 2020. https://www.bbc.com/news/world-asia-india-52176564.

Business Standard. (2020). *Business Standard* [Online]. Accessed August 2020. https://www.business-standard.com/article/current-affairs/Covid-19-impact-50-of-global-youth-depressed-17-out-of-jobs-says-ilo-120081200580_1.html.

Deshingkar, P., & Akter, S. (2009). Migration and human development in India. *Human Development Research Paper (HDRP) Series, 13*.

GOI. (2017). *Youth in India*. MOSPI.

India, G. O. (2020). *MOHFW* [Online]. https://www.mohfw.gov.in/.

Khanna, A. (2020). Impact of migration of labour force due to global COVID-19 pandemic with reference to India. *Journal of Health Management, 22*(2), 181–191.

Kumar, A., Nayar, K. R., & Bhat, L. D. (2020). Debate: COVID-19 and children in India. *Child and Adolescent Mental Health, 25*(3), 165–166.

Kumar, S., Kumar, D., Christopher, B., & Doss, C. (2020). The rise and impact of COVID-19 in India. *Frontiers in Medicine, 7*, 250.

Kumaran, M. (2012). *Leadership in libraries: A focus on ethnic-minority librarians*. Cambridge: Woodhead Publishing (Oxford).

Lexa, F. J. (2017). Principled leadership. In *Leadership lessons for health care providers* (pp. 172–176).

Pescosolido, B. (2011). The sociology of social networks. In *The Handbook of 21st Century Sociology* (pp. 208–217).

Pettiwala, F. (2020). *Economic times* [Online]. Accessed July 2020. https://economictimes.indiatimes.com/jobs/view-indian-youth-can-revitalise-Covid-battered-economy/articleshow/76691975.cms.

Ranjana, C. (2020). COVID 19 pandemic: Mental health challenges of internal migrant workers of India. *Asian Journal of Psychiatry, 54*, 1–4.

Sengupta, S., & Jha, M. K. (2020). Social policy, COVID-19 and impoverished migrants: Challenges and prospects in locked down India. *The International Journal of Community and Social Development, 2*(2), 152–172.

Suchman, E. (1964). Sociomedical variations among ethnic groups. *American Journal of Sociology, 70*(3), 319–331.

Sudevan, P. (2020). *The Hindu* [Online]. Accessed May 2020. https://www.thehindu.com/sci-tech/technology/why-elearning-is-not-a-sustainable-solution-to-the-Covid19-education-crisis-in-india/article31560007.ece.

Tiwari, S. (2020). *IndiaSpend* [Online]. Accessed June 2020. https://www.indiaspend.com/india-spent-1-of-gdp-on-public-health-for-15-years-result-is-vulnerability-to-crises/.

TOI. (2020). *The Times of India* [Online]. https://timesofindia.indiatimes.com/india/41-lakh-youth-lose-jobs-in-india-due-to-Covid-19-impact-ilo-adb-report/articleshow/77624585.cms.

Trading Economics. (2020). *Trading Economics*. [Online]. https://tradingeconomics.com/india/unemployment-rate

UN. (2020). *United Nations* [Online]. Accessed July 2020. https://www.un.org/en/sections/issues-depth/youth-0/.

Wasserman, S., & Faust, K. (1994). *Social network analysis: Methods and applications* (Vol. 8). Cambridge University Press.

WHO. (2020). *World Health Organization* [Online]. http://www.emro.who.int/health-topics/corona-virus/questions-and-answers.html.

Zeitlyn, B., Deshingkar, P., & Holtom, B. (2014). Internal and regional migration for construction work: A research agenda. Migrating out of poverty RPC.

# 6 Women's Movements in Turkey

## Patriarchal Authoritarianism from Empire to Republic

*Fresia Sabeti and Mohsen Moheimany*

### Introduction

The patriarchal, authoritarian state in Turkey, both during the Ottoman and the Republic eras, used different legal and political measures that effectively pushed back the progressive direction of the women's rights movements. One of the main factors that have affected the political environment and scope of action for women leaders and activists in civil society is the state's linkage with the West.

While during the three waves of democratisation in the 19th and 20th centuries, several countries experienced large-scale shifts in their political systems, including leadership, structure, policies, groups, and culture, in the second half of the 20th century, several other countries underwent reform-based political and economic shifts across East Europe, the Middle East, and South America (Huntington, 1996; Levitsky & Way, 2010). However, critical studies argue that many of these shifts and reforms were not genuine, because they did not succeed in establishing stable democratic institutions and even reversed towards new authoritarianism in the following decades (Cavatorta & Durac, 2015; Norton, 1996).

In a study of authoritarian and hybrid regimes, Levitsky and Way (2010) highlighted the notion of linkage and leverage concerning the relationships between undemocratic countries and the West, in particular Europe. They discuss that after the decline of Communism, the linkage of several authoritarian regimes with the West grew, and subsequently increased the leverage of the global actors, including the United States, the European Union, international organisations like the United Nations, NGOs, and media upon the politics of authoritarian regimes. The mentioned study (2010, p. 88) emphasises the unique role of the European Union and its membership negotiations with a number of courtiers, markedly regarding its 'commitment to democracy' as a key criterion for membership. The

DOI: 10.4324/9781003288145-6

EU required the interested countries to have stable democratic institutions, the rule of law, and respect for human rights and minorities. In the 1960s, these criteria were the reasons for not accepting Greece and Portugal, and it has remained a significant factor for excluding Turkey (Levitsky & Way, 2010, p. 87). The issue of membership and relations with the EU has determined the situation for the social movements inside Turkey during the last decades.

When it comes to linkage with the West and international organisations, the authoritarian leaders not only have had political and economic interests, but also receiving international encouragement, prestige, and funds are further incentives for them to implement a series of liberalisations. The post-1980s political reforms in the Middle East and North Africa brought some structural shifts, which included decentralisation of power and growth of young civil societies and movements inside the countries (Clement, 2010; Fawcett & Daugbjerg, 2012; Bergh, 2012). But most economic reforms and liberalisations, such as privatisation of public sector services, soon turned out to be selective and engineered that provided the states and leaders with further legal and political instruments and mechanisms for expanding patron-client networks (Heydemann, 2010; Smoke, 2001). While new groups and leaders, including women, rose and grew in the form of NGOs, the control over institutional adjustments remained in the hands of the rulers and even provided them with more opportunities to recruit civil society leaders and groups (Bergh, 2012; Vráblíková, 2014).

In a study on the post-1980s Arab world, Heydemann (2010) states that apart from repression, authoritarian leaders also resort to planting and growing docile forces in civil society. He points to a number of countries such as Syria and Jordan, where the families of leaders and state figures set up non-transparent organisations with the title of non-governmental organisations. Arab leaders used these loyal groups as the mechanisms of distributing state funds and public resources among citizens and forces to co-opt them and reduce the effectiveness of societal forces. The women movements are not an exception to this. Women forces may help rulers keep the status quo, either intentionally or unintentionally by playing according to the formal rules and informal practices set by authoritarian regimes (Clarke, 1998; Fowler, 1993; Brownlee, 2002).

The trajectory of the women movements in Turkey shows a pattern of ever-developing authoritarianism that smartly used a set of measures to implant loyalism, impose patriarchalism, and contain critical women movements. This trajectory became more complicated in the 21st century, as the following sections discuss.

## Rising with the Westernisation

Despite being a Sunni majority country, the secular-oriented reforms of the Ottoman Empire during the 'Adjustment period' (1839–1876), triggered modernisation of the state apparatus and the social system, which brought about the earliest formal civil liberties for different strata, including women. During this period, affected by the waves of women's uprisings in the West, the Turkish women movement started to appear and grow. This came with legal developments, as after the proclamation of the First Constitution in 1876, Ottoman women increased their vibrancy and social presence as well as broadened the spectrum of their demands (çakır, 1996). Following several decades of reform, by the proclamation of the Second Constitution in 1908, the first groups of forerunner women were given a chance in the state apparatus as they were employed by the Ottoman administration from 1913, as well as study at a women's university. This meant the rise of social or political women as leaders happened by the will of the emperor. The cohort of women leaders and activists in this period had a range of different identities and backgrounds including Roman, Kurdish, Armenian, and Jewish; but, after the establishment of the Republic in 1923, nationalist rulers sought to create a monolingual, mono-ideological Turkish-Muslim system and in doing that they tried to manipulate the composition of the women social forces (Berber, 2017a, 2017b).

In the Republic era, legal modernisation and cultural westernisation continued but took the women's movement and female leaders into a different trajectory. Under Mustafa Kemal Ataturk's nationalist government, the Family Law Decree that had been passed in 1917 was still practised as it was the only legal reference outlining some of the women's rights. As for associationism, the 'People's Women's Sect' was formed by a number of forerunner women as one of the earliest leading groups by the leading role of Nazih Mohiuddin. The central demand of this group was inspired by the first wave of feminism that was simply about gender equality in laws and politics. However, due to the non-recognition of women's political rights in the Family Law Decree, the authoritative government did not allow the movement to develop organisations and form a political party. Later, when the Constitution was amended, the group succeeded in setting up the Turkish Women's Alliance as a party in 1924, which was a step forward for women (Zihinoğlu, 2003).

With further legal and political shifts, such as the introduction of the Turkish Civil Code, and finally as a result of the push and demands of feminist activists in 1926, more particular rights were given to women (Ozcurumez & Cengiz, 2011). For example, male monogamy was abandoned, gender equality was formalised in court testimony, inheritance, and divorce laws, and the right to education and employment were incorporated in the body of civil laws. These were the foundations of future civic movements. Following these shifts, with the acquisition of civil rights, women chanted for appeals in the political spheres, and with the gradual reforms in 1934, they eventually gained the right to vote and to enter the parliament as a representative. This formally brought them into politics.

In the 1940s and 1950s, the increase in the Turkish government's tendency towards the West improved women associationism, for example, the Turkish Association of University Women and the Society for the Protection of the Rights of Women was formed (Cagaptay, 2007). However, the growth of women movement organisations was under the control and mandate of the authoritative state, which concluded in the prevalence of state-backed movements, a movement that while it increased women's public presence and activities, ignored their private life, and certain concepts such as 'motherhood inside the home' and 'devoted chastity' remained influential (White, 2003). The rights that were given by women were labelled as the 'gifts of the Republic'.

In the 1980s, although some restrictive policies were undergoing against opposition groups and politicians and also multiple coups of the military took place, women were still able to join the second wave of feminism, though with a decade delay. This wave came as a response to the deficits of equalitarian waves and sought shifts beyond political and social equality (Ozcurumez & Cengiz, 2011). While this movement politically took a critical position against the authoritarianism of Kemalism, it used a more critical approach and opposed the 'objectivity' assigned to women by the ruling elites (Tekeli, 1995).

In this period, the notion of 'rebellious' feminism was transferred to Turkey, and the emerging independent feminist leaders did not confine themselves to legal rights anymore (Çubukçu, 2004; Berber, 2017a, 2017b). Also, the leading groups of women brought their focus from the nation, cast, or human rights issues to their own rights and status, for example, in May 1987, three thousand women marched on Istanbul streets to protest domestic physical violence. Moreover, following the introduction of the 'Decade for Women' by the United Nations in 1975, the women's movement in Turkey could revive, as forerunner female academics and writers formed several small associations and organisations. Turkey's first feminist publishing house, established in 1983, was a milestone for women in this decade.

After the announcement of 1975 as the World Year of Women by the United Nations, an international meeting of women started being held every five years to review operational plans and analyse the progress in the field. Turkey joined the Convention on the Elimination of All Forms of Discrimination Against Women towards the end of the Women Decade in 1985. The Turkish women's movement prepared a petition urging the government to take immediate and proper actions to implement the convention, which had been in force since March 1986. It was welcomed unexpectedly by the society, as 6,000 signatures went on the petition. This was the first mass movement of women since 1980, and after this campaign, the 'Association for the Elimination of Discrimination against Women' was established to bring the provisions of the convention into domestic law.

In the 1990s, in addition to the establishment of new organisations and associations, many women with competing political ideologies and ethnic identities found a chance to engage in effective dialogues in the public sphere. More amendments took place in civil laws, criminal laws, and even the Constitution. As a result, women were reaping what they had sown over the past two decades (Berber, 2017a, 2017b). In parallel, the coordination of the ruling government with international organisations' agendas in this field, specifically the United Nations and the European Union, accelerated women's activism and rights. However, the phenomenon of 'project feminism' dominated the feminist movements because many feminist leaders and groups focused on implementing international projects. This decade could be called the decade of the manifestation of feminism in Turkey that was reflected in the spreading discourse of feminism among the masses (Berber, 2017a, 2017b).

## Falling with the Failure of European Membership

Women movements in Turkey gradually went into a different trajectory when conservative neoliberalism became prominent in the country during the rise of Erdogan to power as Prime Minister through the 2002 elections. His original manifesto was a conservative democratic one that sought liberalisation of politics (Hurriyet, 2001). However, later and by the consolidation of the Justice and Development Party (AKP) in the administration and parliament, the country experienced a turn towards a new era of authoritarianism in terms of discourse, laws, and political processes (Karaveli, 2016).

In the early years of its governance, AKP kept its predecessors' trend of joining the European Union, which came with an open politics and created some space for the secular and feminist women activists. The reforms during Erdogan's incumbency as Prime Minister brought in several shifts in relation to women's civil and political rights with upgrades in the Civil Code (2001), the Criminal Code (2004), and the Constitution. Among the legal amendments was the introduction of Article 10 of the Constitution in May 2004, stating 'men and women have equal rights, and the government must ensure that equality is achieved'. Also, in October

2005, the MPs from the Republican People's Party (CHP) in the parliament set up the Commission for the Investigation of Honour killing and Family Murders, a long-standing issue concerning the safety of women. Moreover, public supports were given to associations, foundations, and NGOs related to women's issues coincided with the rise of traditional and modern NGOs up to about 150,000 in 2018 (TUSEV, 2011). The ministries funded and cooperated with international organisations, e.g., UNICEF, in raising several campaigns with pro-women titles such as 'Girls should come to school' and 'Daddy, take me to school' to support the right to education for women. Yet, in the formal manifesto and discourse of the ruling party, and the prime minister himself, women were and still are defined as individuals who should foremost nurture future generations from home, an NGO leader said in her personal interview. Thus, even in this period, the status of gender equality measures in political participation was not appropriate.

As both the new feminist movement and the ruling party consolidated their position and heightened their expectations, oppositely, almost by the beginning of the second decade of the 21st century, both sides gradually clashed with one another, and tensions increased between them. One major reason was that the policies of the government at the international level did not succeed as expected, with Erdogan's dream of joining the EU seeming to fail (Sociais, 2018).

In society, the rhetoric of feminist leaders was no longer limited to demanding legal reforms and implementing women-empowerment projects. Instead, due to the increase in public access to social media and under the influence of global feminism, the Turkish women's-rights movement spread across the country from Istanbul and also ethnic-feminist sects and leaders became more active and competed with the government's nationalist ideology. An instance of this was Kurdish-language slogans in women's rallies in Istanbul and Ankara, the most important of which was 'Jin, Jian, Azadi' meaning 'woman, life, and freedom.' The rise of new ethnic, identity, gender, and ideological demands in women movements reduced the unity between women leaders in some fields, but at the same time challenged the government on more political and geographical fronts. An experienced woman activist said in a personal interview that in the second decade of the current century, the composition of the Turkish feminist movement changed and comprised of a new cohort of women, youths, and human rights activists who challenge the Turkish repressive political system and its unjust economic and legal order, with dozens of ethnic, queer, and eco-vegan organisations within it.

As for the political regime, towards 2010, the rotation of power became limited both within the state and the ruling party, with the Erdogan administration shifting towards radical Islamic authoritarianism in the discourse and policy approaches (Gongu, 2009).

In terms of discourse, while in 2000 Erdogan had referred to the necessity of reviving women's freedoms and fighting ignorance, and admitted to the fact that the Turkish government had 'ignored women'; later in 2013, he changed his stance explicitly to an anti-modern right and stated that female students should not live together with the opposite sex in a shared house (BBC Turk, 2013). The Erdogan administration also targeted women's social and private lives as well as different sects of women movements including LGBTs by associating them with 'terrorist organisations' that have no moral values (VOA, 2021). In his AKP party, Boland Arinc, a senior member and then Deputy Prime Minister, said in a 2014 public speech: 'a woman should be chaste, and distinguish the mahram (intimate) from the non-mahram (non-intimate), and not laugh out loudly in public'.

As for policies and practices, the government officially prioritised the family as the key institution over women as individuals. Just imagine renaming the Ministry of Women and Family Affairs to the Ministry of Family and Social Policy in 2011, which feminists interpreted as revealing that the policies of AKP were not in favour of women any longer. The Erdogan administration and AKP also have been seeking to contain the rights and freedoms that had been reclaimed by the modern women's movement. On the one hand, population growth became a priority – which defines women as its human forces, and on the other hand, efforts to criminalise abortion brought the focus on the role of women in reproduction.

Laws concerning women's rights and participation were targeted by the administration's Islamic-oriented interpretations (Ayata & Dogangun, 2017; Gungordu, 2019). Just consider the end of the second decade, when after ten years of signing the CoE by his order, in 2021, Erdogan withdrew from it, despite the public discontent.

The gender policy of the ruling AKP, when needed, resorted to more forceful measures to maintain power, as well as imposing and disseminating its discourse on the media (Gungordu, 2019). While in the first decade of the 2000s, AKP had the policy of freeing media organisations from the monopoly of the state, in the following years, any political tensions in Turkey led to the suppression of the opposition media and the arrest of independent vocal journalists. This spread fear in the women movement media too, as the ethnic media and activists had been somehow integrated into women movements more than before (Ozvarıs, 2020). The arrests and detentions mostly targeted writers and journalists who criticised the party's religious conservatism, with more than 120 journalists in jail in 2019 (Reuters, 2019).

The shifts in the government gender-related policies came with regressive changes in the status of violence against women. According to the Platform to End Crime Against Women, while in 2010, 180 women were killed by men, mostly the ones close to them, this number rose to 300 in 2020 as stricter measures have been used against critical women forces (KCDP, 2021).

In parallel, the ruling elite and their relatives gradually expanded their presence in the civil society to control it from the inside. In March 2013, the President's daughter, Somayeh Erdogan, founded the Women and Democracy Foundation (Kadem), whose mission, in line with the government's discourse, was working on the production of a new discourse about women. Moreover, the authorities set up many other state-funded organisations to produce and disseminate the state's conservative discourse of replacing the universal concept of gender justice with the Islamic-oriented concept of gender equality (Bodur Un, 2021). At the same time, controversial issues such as abortion became subject to state defamation campaigns. Erdogan repeatedly called abortion 'murder' in his official speeches and also labelled the women without children 'incomplete' (The Guardian, 2016).

To contain and nullify the societal pressures, the government increased discrimination between critical and loyal groups (Gonzales, 2016). This was sought for through redistribution of grants and funds. In one camp, in the cohort of equalitarian women, groups and leaders have been supported by international organisations, for instance, in 2021 the EU and UN launched a three-year project to allocate funds to NGOs to promote women's rights (Daily Sabah, 2021). Inside the country, NGOs such as the Foundation for the Support of Civic Institutions to Support Gender Equality in Turkey facilitated international funds for local groups. But, in the opposite camp, organisations affiliated with the AKP and the loyal groups, such as Kadem, sourced their income from outstanding members who are mostly high-ranking women in the AKP, or the family members of statemen. This made the ground of activism unjust between the two camps. A member of 'Purple Union' NGO said in a personal interview: 'We cannot financially compete with the state-supported NGO Kadem, but money is not everything, because, after a political shift, Kadem will disappear as it has no ideological backing, whereas we will survive since we are the ones against masculinity'.

The women-unfriendly policies of the state faced a more radical approach by critical women leaders. The state measure and rhetoric against abortion brought women activists to nationwide protests, an important one of which was the 'Gezi Park' protest in 2013. The protesters chanted slogans such as 'my body, my right' that resonated broadly on social media and as a reaction to the growing authority of the state not only over the agency of women but also over their bodies. The murder of a female university student named Ozgecan Aslan in 2015 also provoked organised action of feminist women against increasing violence.

## Coup, Covid, and Growing Securitisation

The authoritarian tendency of the Turkish administration accelerated from the 2016 attempted coup and it tightened the space of activism for different sects of women movements, such as the LGBT and Kurdish activists. Having decided to concentrate much more power in his hands, Erdogan pushed forward a change in the constitution in 2017 and shifted the political system from parliamentarian to presidential, with which the level of direct intervention and power of the government in non-state activism increased. For instance, at the end of 2020, the administration passed a bill in the parliament which aimed at controlling the financing of NGOs with the flag of combating money laundering and terrorism. It provoked a reaction from vocal groups, as 520 NGOs, including women's organisations, objected to the policy by a way of a statement, but the government continued the restrictive policies (DW, 2020). Also, the administration issued an executive order that legalised the intervention of the state in appointing NGOs' presidents whenever the authorities would suspect an NGO's activities being related to terrorism. In confronting women movements, terrorism so far has been a pretext to take down opposition groups and individuals. In Erdogan's discourse terrorism refers to any action against state and territorial security. Moreover, by the pretext of the coup, the arresting, imprisoning, and sentencing increased as tens of thousands of people were targeted from several sections including state and non-state (Vonberg et al., 2017).

In 2020, the outbreak of Covid-19 and the national crisis due to the pandemic worsened the general situation of women and particularly for women's-rights groups and activists. In March 2021, the annual index of Gender Gap, published by the World Economic Forum, showed the declining status of Turkey. This country fell from 105th in 2006 to 133rd in 2021 (World Economic Forum, 2021). Moreover, reports showed an increase in the number of honour killings. A survey by the United Nation showed a similar trend of losing jobs by women in Turkey, as well as an exacerbation of women's disadvantages (Daily Sabah, 2020). This situation concerned women's rights leaders and groups about the rights of living and basic safety for women and girls, more than anything else. Simultaneously, because of lockdowns and public restrictions, the government has had a strong excuse in hand to cancel, repress, or confront any public action of the women who aimed at organising a protest. In this environment, the Erdogan administration could advance its anti-women policies more easily. The abandoning of the Istanbul Convention by the Erdogan Administration is just an instance of this.

Consequently, it seemed that from 2010 to 2020 women's-rights leaders and groups had to step back gradually and eventually give up many of their efforts for the bigger goal of saving basic rights.

## Conclusion

The second decade of the 21st century has been a turning point for women's-rights movements in Turkey as the republic increased patriarchalism, alongside its nationalist ideology. It triggered an upgrade in state authoritarianism that led to more social crises, more violence, and fewer rights and safety for women.

The Turkish government in the last century used a set of measures and resources, particularly state machinery, to first grow a cohort of women leaders and groups but subsequently seek to engineer the composition, demands, and discourse of the women movement. This shift in the recent decades came after a period of purge in the state, which was the result of the consolidation of Erdogan's camp in power. By stepping towards a 'police state,' the Turkish regime used the methods of repressing outspoken women, and at almost the same time closing and revoking the licence of leading feminist groups.

The greatest challenge women face currently seems to be the severe conservatism of the rulers. From 2015 onwards, the combination of Islamic discourse and authoritarian practices of the state concretely restricted the women critical forces and lowered their expectations because their basic rights had been curtailed, while maybe feminists' voices has still been heard more thanks to social media. While the state succeeded in dispersing and isolating the leading feminist figures and groups, still women's issues are significant in society. Women can still organise protests and when this happens, the number of participants is considerable. Leaders and activists point out that the women movement is still the most influential in terms of mobilising people on the streets and influencing public opinion since the women's worsening situation has become very visible and tangible for ordinary citizens.

## References

Ayata, A. G., & Dogangun, G. (2017). Gender politics of the AKP: Restoration of a religio-conservative gender climate. *Journal of Balkan and Near Eastern Studies, 19*(6), 610–623.

BBC Turkce. (2013, October 5). *Erdoğan'dan Öğrenci Evi Açıklaması.* https://www.bbc.com/turkce/haberler/2013/11/131105_erdogan_ogrenci_ev.

Berber, N. (2017a, September 18). *OSMANLI'DAN TÜRKİYE CUMHURİYETİ'NE KADIN HAREKETİ.* HEİNRİCH-BÖLL-STİFTUNG. https://tr.boell.org/tr/2017/09/18/osmanlidan-turkiye-cumhuriyetine-kadin-hareketi

Berber, N. (2017b, September 18). *1980'ler: Feminist Hareket Yeniden....* HEİNRİCH-BÖLL-STİFTUNG. https://tr.boell.org/tr/2017/09/18/1980ler-feminist-hareket-yeniden

Bergh, S. (2012). Introduction: Researching the effects of neoliberal reforms on local governance in the southern mediterranean. *Mediterranean Politics, 17*(3), 303–321.

Bodur Un, M. (2021). From "gender equality" to "gender justice". De-Europeanization of gender equality policies in Turkey. In A. Bilgin (Ed.), *EU/Turkey relations in the shadow of crisis* (pp. 133–154). Lexington Books.

Brownlee, J. M. (2002). Low tide after the third wave: Exploring politics under authoritarianism. *Comparative Politics, 34*(4), 477–498.

Cakir, S. (1996). *Osmanlı Kadın Hareketi.* Metis Yayınları.

Cagaptay, A. (2007). *Secularism and foreign policy in Turkey: New elections, troubling trends.* The Washington Institute for Near East Policy.

Cavatorta, F., & Durac, V. (2015). *Politics and governance in the Middle East.* Palgrave.

Clarke, G. (1998). Non-governmental organizations (NGOs) and politics in the developing countries. *Journal of Political Studies, 46*(1), 36–52.

Clement, M. H. (2010). Autoritarismes démocratique et démocraties autoritaires au XXIe siècle: Convergences Nord-Sud. Mélanges offerts à Michel Camau, and: Démocraties et authoritarismes: Fragmentation et hybridation des régimes (review). *The Middle East Journal, 64*(2), 316–318.

Daily Sabah. (2020, August 5). *COVID-19 accentuates women's disadvantage in Turkey's labour market, UN survey shows.* Retrieved April 2021, from Daily Sabah: https://www.dailysabah.com/business/economy/covid-19-accentuates-womens-disadvantage-in-turkeys-labor-market-un-survey-shows.

Daily Sabah. (2021, June). *EU, UN to fund NGOs for women's rights in Turkey.* Retrieved from Daily Sabah: https://www.dailysabah.com/turkey/eu-un-to-fund-ngos-for-womens-rights-in-turkey/news.

DW. (2020, December 20). *520 STK'dan yeni yasa teklifine karşı ortak bildiri.* Retrieved from Deutsche Welle: https://www.dw.com/tr/520-stkdan-yeni-yasa-teklifine-kar%C5%9F%C4%B1-ortak-bildiri/a-56052504.

Fawcett, P., & Daugbjerg, C. (2012). Explaining governance outcomes: Epistemology, network governance and policy network. *Political Studies Review, 10*, 195–207.

Fowler, A. (1993). Non-governmental organizations as agents of democratization: An African perspective. *Journal of International Development, 5*(3), 325–339.

Gonzales, N. (2016). The feminist movement during the AKP era in Turkey: Challenges and opportunities. *Middle Eastern Studies, 52*(2), 198–214.

Gungordu, S. E. (2019). AKP Döneminde Biyopolitik Stratejiler. *AKP DÖNEMİNDE TÜRKİYE'DE BİYOPOLİTİK YÖNELİMLER: KÜRTAJ POLİTİKALARI ÜZERİNE BİR İNCELEME.* Ankara, Ankara, Turkey.

Heydemann, S. (2010, October). Upgrading authoritarianism in the Arab World. *The Saban Centre for Middle East Policy, 13*. The Brookings Institution.

Huntington, S. P. (1996). *Political order in changing societies*. Yale University Press.

Hurriyet. (2001, August 14). *Adalet ve Kalkınma Partisi kuruldu*. Retrieved from Hürriyet: https://www.hurriyet.com.tr/gundem/adalet-ve-kalkinma-partisi-kuruldu-10017.

İçduygu, A., Meydanoğlu, Z., & Sert, D. Ş. (2011). Civil society in Turkey: At a turning point. TUSEV, CIVICUS civil society index (CSI) project country report for Turkey II. *TUSEV Publications*, 19–179.

Karaveli, H. (2016). Erdogan's journey: Conservatism and authoritarianism in Turkey. *Foreign Affairs, 95*(6), 121–130.

KCDP. (2021, July 8). *Kadın Cinayetlerini Durduracağız Platformu*. Retrieved from Kadın Cinayetlerini: http://kadincinayetlerinidurduracagiz.net/kategori/veriler.

Levitsky, S., & Way, L. A. (2010). *Competitive authoritarianism: Hybrid regimes after the cold war*. Cambridge University Press.

Norton, A. R. (1996). *Civil society in the Middle East*. Koninklijke.

Ozcurumez, S., & Cengiz, F. S. (2011). On resilience and response beyond value change: Transformation of women's movement in post-1980 Turkey. *Women's Studies International Forum, 34*(1), 20–30.

Ozvarış, H. (2020, May 26). *Otoriterleşen AKP İktidarında Türkiye Medyasının Dönüşümü*. Retrieved from red thread: https://red-thread.org/otoriterlesen-akp-iktidarinda-turkiye-medyasinin-donusumu/.

Reuters. (2019, November). *More than 120 journalists still jailed in Turkey: International press institute*. Retrieved from Reuters: https://www.reuters.com/article/us-turkey-security-media-idUSKBN1XT26T

Smoke, P. (2001). *Overview of decentralization and workshop theme linkage. The participatory symposium*. UNCDF.

Sociais, A. (2018). Populism and competitive authoritarianism in Turkey. *Southeast European and Black Sea Studies, 18*(4), 467–487.

The Guardian. (2016, June 6). *Turkish president says childless women are 'deficient, incomplete'*. Retrieved from The Guardian: https://www.theguardian.com/world/2016/jun/06/turkish-president-erdogan-childless-women-deficient-incomplete.

VOA. (2021, February 4). *Turkey's Erdogan calls student protesters terrorists, intensifying anti-LGBT rhetoric*. Retrieved from VOA: https://www.voanews.com/extremism-watch/turkeys-erdogan-calls-student-protesters-terrorists-intensifying-anti-lgbt-rhetoric.

Vonberg, J., Said-Moorhouse, L., & Fox, K. (2017, April). *47,155 arrests: Turkey's post-coup crackdown by the numbers*. Retrieved from CNN: https://edition.cnn.com/2017/04/14/europe/turkey-failed-coup-arrests-detained/index.html.

Vráblíková, K. (2014). How context matters? Mobilization, political ppportunity structures, and nonelectoral political participation in old and new democracies. *Comparative Political Studies, 47*(2), 203–229.

White, J. B. (2003). State feminism, modernization, and the Turkish republican woman. *NWSA Journal, 15*(3), 145–159.

World Economic Forum. (2021, March 31). *Global gender gap report 2021*. World Economic Forum.

Zihinoglu, Y. (2003). *Kadınsız İnkılap Nezihe Muhiddin, Kadınlar Halk Fırkası, Kadın Birliği*. Metis Yayınları.

# 7 The Tale of Reformism in Iran

*Nader Ganji*

## Introduction

In the late 19th-century Iran, feudalism was breathing its last. This was a new era in the Qajar dynasty since with the development of capitalism, the formation of the bourgeoisie was initiated. Nonetheless, confusion and dispersion within the society led to the emergence of various factions, each of which responded differently to such a transformation. One of these factions was reformism which was not only a conflict of thoughts among divergent social strata or simply an outcome of the theoretical attempts of groups or individuals as it is often claimed but rather a tendency within the bourgeoisie which gradually grew with the expansion of universal capitalism. Most scholars have emphasised the influence of the European political thoughts on the formation of such movements and neglected major factions fighting for their interests (Abrahamian, 1979).

Contrary to the situation in Europe, capitalism in Iran was established and continued the process of its domination through an alliance with the ruling feudal system and the upper faction of the emerging bourgeoisie. Although the reformists were affected by intellectualism, reformism in Iran had a reactionary and conservative nature. This is mostly because the new bourgeoisie was unable to control social riots or compete with their world rivals. Neither had it the economic or political capacity to step aside in favour of the labour. Thereby, it had to intensify the current dictatorship and control the religion's leverage as religious doctrines may build commitment to the movement, and introduce the strategy of protest (Ganz, 2010; Morris & Staggenborg, 2004). For this reason, the main characteristic of the Iranian reformers' leadership, who could inspire or organise masses to participate in movements, was conservatism and religiosity. For instance, different groups could be easily mobilised by one camp by provoking their religious emotions (Foran, 1993).

Furthermore, reformism in practice was embarked on with letter writing, petitioning, and taking sanctuary in sacred places, and historically, the more it expanded, the more it employed a religious identity (Ashraf, 1980: 107–8). In the Qajar dynasty, letter writing to the Shahs became a common activity (see, e.g., Abdolamin, 2019). They succeeded in dismissing a few officials including Prime Minister Ain al-Dawla and establishing a house of justice, both in 1906 (Enayat, 2013). Nonetheless, with riots being widespread, these factions ultimately had to reach a compromise with the rulers. In Europe, the bourgeoisie, before establishing government and strengthening its social and political power, was already economically dominant and later became politically dominant too. In Iran, however, before becoming economically dominant, they allied with the state. As important is another factual feature of reformism which was the necessity to be part of the political power structure. Because otherwise, this movement would have lost its strength of influence, as it lacked strong social bases in the masses. This stream has rather ridden on the protests of the masses in different periods under the name of democracy while grabbing Islam and using people as a springboard to political power. Morris and Staggenborg (2004) highlight that the leaders of such movements are mostly from the middle and upper classes. Nevertheless, they neglect that the choice of the masses has been only limited to deciding who in the bourgeoisie class should represent them as leaders. This is even more valid in the case of Iran, in the absence of clear demands from the masses, and where the society lacked organised movements.

Admittedly, since the masses lack the capability of understanding such struggles, leaders have a vital role in radical social movements (Marx & Engels, 1968). While social movement theory would greatly benefit by taking into account the roles of both agency and structural conditions (see, e.g., Morris & Staggenborg, 2004), where the political system is historically incapable of meeting the demands of the movements, the need for analysing the structure may be highlighted. Hence, it was not merely the social leaders that shaped reformism in Iran, but also and more importantly, the capital position that predominated the agents. This does not imply that leaders do not possess influence, but that movements' success or failure highly depends on the changes in capital structure, especially when the state capacity is weak.

## Reformism and Constitutional Revolution (1905–1911)

The emerging Iranian bourgeoisie could be categorised into three main broad factions. The upper consisted of feudists, state officials, courtiers, and mainstream clergy that already held core power. The middle included merchants, low-ranking clerics, and intelligentsia. They were middle in terms of their position to political power, their status was mostly peripheral and their mottos mainly included reformism, liberalism, and nationalism. The lower, however, was less affected by Western thoughts and considering their marginal role in power or their minor share in public property, their conflict was clearer. They were predominantly supporting the communist bloc and were thought of as being anti-imperialists. This faction was seeking an independent national bourgeoisie and a greater role in the political economy for the labour as opposed to the comprador bourgeoisie.

The upper faction was completely conservative, while the middle was seeking reform, while the lower looked forward to overthrowing the system to establish a form of the governmental bourgeoisie. Nevertheless, communal divisions in Iran not only acted as a barrier to gaining power by middle and lower factions but also allowed the upper faction to dominate the country in that period (Abrahamian, 1979). Thus, the growing dominance of the bourgeois came about by political power and took place by the hand of the first faction which was maintaining its sovereignty. It took a long time for the bourgeoisie to get political power in the West, whereas in Iran the situation was different. Feudalists became the new bourgeois, and no real collapse of feudalism happened. In Europe, feudalists almost completely lost their power while they merged into the emerging class in Iran.

The factions that had no share in property and profit and could not establish a partnership with the British through new concessions were left behind (e.g., Reuter, 1889 and D'Arcy, 1901). Meanwhile, however, the upper faction maintained its superior status and easily conquered most capital share and profitable and golden areas through new contracts and monopolies. It later suppressed its rivals thanks to these privileges. Therefore, it was the government alongside the upper faction that took the lead in designing and implementing its ideal political, legal, and civil structure and seizing both political and economic opportunities. Indeed, the government is only an instrument of ruling for one class, a conception that is often neglected in the literature (Poulantzas, 1973). Hence, it is unsurprising that those other factions soon became dissatisfied with their situation.

While the middle faction emphasised legislative reforms and the rule of law, it did not take long for their campaign to take a rebellious form (Katouzian, 2021). This faction was dissatisfied with the upper streams holding different means to establish their dominance. Moreover, it is not clear whether they were reformists in the first place. They gradually became reformists as they could not tolerate the domination of capital by the upper one, their low status, and a minor role in the political structure. Their way of opposing for years, however, was peaceful opposition-building, with the discourse of reformism, and they had enough reasons for conflicting with the dominant faction.

The inferior faction was suffering the pressure of the upper faction. They had a stronger tie with the masses and could mobilise them much more efficiently than the other two especially with regard to occupying streets and running demonstrations (Abrahamian, 1968). They saw this form of capitalism in contrast to their romanticist ambitions and, therefore, chanted independent and national industrialisation as their utopia. For this reason, they felt they were enemies of the other factions and accused them of betrayal and cheating, and labelled their leaders the agents of imperialism or manipulated puppets of the imperialist powers. Nonetheless, even this lower faction remained silent during the protests of the peasantry. Emerging bourgeoisie alongside old feudalists widely suppressed social protests of the masses. We need look no further than the Battle of Fort Tabarsi (1848–1849) or the Babism movements, where all these factions were absent. These happened under the conditions that the development of capitalism was still going through its first phases. The first and the middle later formed a partnership in the political structure, although only when dispersion happened within the ruling class could the reformists come to power.

## From Constitutional Revolution to the Reza Shah's Coup (1905–1921)

Reformist movements took place not only in Iran but also in many parts of Asia such as Russia, China, East Asian countries, and almost all the societies that were experiencing the same process (Keddie, 1962). Inbound capital flows commenced from the reign of Nasser-al-din Shah brought about different factions struggling for power and capital. However, there is a tendency to constrain this factionalism to only ideological thoughts. By way of illustration, the struggle between Ayatollah Nayini and Sheikh Fazlollah Nuri was not over the concepts of *Mashrute and Mashru'e* (Constitutionalism versu Religious State). There were two main rival leaders of the protests amid the Revolution (1905–1911) whose conflict should not be limited to thoughts as it was rather a quarrel between the representatives of developing capitalism and collapsing feudalism. In other words, thoughts and beliefs are the verbal expressions of a struggle that was materialistically running between these factions.

While the state-backed upper faction was signing contracts with the West and making profits, reformers were seeking a democracy-like form of government. Democracy, formation of parliament, rule of law, election, and civil society were the ideals which this faction focused on, although they gained far less than they demanded. Only in this way could they penetrate power and all other ways were blocked. Indeed, all the intellectuals' demands including democracy and liberalism were replaced with the establishment of a handful of institutions. Nonetheless, while reformism is considered a component of the bourgeoisie, this faction included different streams ranging from nonbelievers and liberals to religious groups and clerics. Therefore, reformism should not be limited to one stratum or guild, not all of whom could elevate their power.

Constitutional Revolution was a milestone in the development of the capitalist mode of production which led to the emergence of factionalism, internal contradictions, and dispersion. Constitutionalism, indeed, was the only solution of the bourgeois to transit from the old relations of feudalism to the new capitalist order. However, the characteristic of reformism in Iran was unique as a different faction, the most religious ones ultimately became the leaders of the movement as they had the historical potential of leadership. Just imagine objections against the Reggie contract or tobacco monopoly during the reign of Nassir-al-Din Shah (see, Keddie, 1966). This was one of the first power exercises of the religious layer for leading later movements, e.g., in the Constitutional Revolution and expanding its power. Many representatives from this faction gradually entered the power structure. But the role of religious groups years later highly affected the subsequent events.

Here again, the lower faction was ignored. The government did not feel the need to fulfil the demands of the labour because they did not exist organisationally, albeit with widespread riots, the turmoil of different factions, and expansion of poverty. That was contrary to Europe, where the proletariat partially met its demands since it had a more powerful social presence. During constitutionalism, the middle faction, through fighting, comprising, and taking sanctuary (led by *ulama* in alliance with merchants) attempted to impose their intended order. The middle faction could get power by establishing parliament and later reformists were born on this ground.

## From Suffocation to Resurgence (1925–1953)

The reign of Reza Shah (1925–1941) can be seen as the solution of the British alongside the upper faction of the bourgeoisie in Iran to settle the related affairs of the process of development of capitalism. On the other hand, it was a period of hegemonising the situation for developing the process of capitalism and maintaining the dominant role of the British capital in other countries such as India. Forming military, police, and security institutions, establishing a strong and centralised government, designing social and political structures appropriate for the new order, weakening tribal chiefs, controlling the area of influence of the feudalists, violently suppressing the emerging labour movement, expanding largely fundamental networks and facilities required for reproduction and accumulation of capital, and suppressing leftist parties were all among the to-do list of the coup in 1921, which led to the establishment of Pahlavi dynasty in 1925. These and much more with regard to preventing social movements to emerge were carried out between the years 1925 and 1941 (Foran, 1993). In doing so, Reza Shah was also struggling with mustiness, political ignorance, and feudalists' petrification, although none of the feudalists could act as a barrier to him.

During this period, the middle faction that represented its identity with liberalism, democracy, and parties' freedom had no place in the new policies and an absolute monarchy had risen from the coup. The first reason was the position of Iran in the universal capitalist labour division and the second was that any form of development of political freedom or formation of a democratic structure would endanger the process of development of capitalism. Iran, indeed, was moving from the old structure and expanding its supremacy to a new era. In this situation, any kind of a non-police-dictatorship could cease the process of domination or be a disturbance. Hence, reformism was on the sideline, and instead, advancement of constitutional ambitions, however limited, took place in alliance with the upper faction including merchants, clerics, and traders, and part of the intellectuals.

With the fall of Reza Shah in 1941 and the occupation of the country by the Allies during World War II, the political structure became unstable, and this provided factions with a new chance again (Ghaffary & Azizimehr, 2015). These factions, under the conditions that different power poles were attempting to reconstruct their status in the hierarchy of global power, reformists in Iran attempted to revive their position too. This revival in the post-Reza Shah era had an essential difference from that of the past. In the past, reformers sought for their existence through democratic and liberalist settlement and compromise with the state or the upper faction, but now they were endeavouring in the hope of establishing democracy, solidification of constitutional monarchy, threatening formal power, forming a nation-state, and expansion of modernism.

## From Coup to Revolution (1953–1979)

Most historians have overemphasised the role of the American and British governments in organising the 1953 coup and focused on the fall of Prime Minister Mosaddeq, outlawing the National Front, and ceasing the process of nationalisation of the oil industry. Nonetheless, it is often neglected that the coup took place during the Cold War. Additionally, the period between 1941 and 1953 was a specific time for Iran both politically and economically as the society had gone through the initial phases of the development of capitalism. Therefore, different parts of the bourgeoisie had contradictory prescriptions and employed different approaches to impose their ideal pattern for the country. Between September 1941 and April 1951, ten prime ministers came to power, none of whom could endure for a long time.

In this situation, Mosaddeq and the National Front came to power while riding on the protests of the masses, while the main role in designing and managing the riots and demonstrations was not played by them, but by the Tudeh Party. Moreover, the reason for the expansion of riots should not be seen in the democratic approach of the National Front, but in dispersion in the Western pole of universal bourgeoisie alongside conflicts among the Iranian bourgeoisie. As important is the effective role of the Soviet Union in its spheres of influence including Iran. Scared of the expansion of communism, the Western pole had no way but to organise a coup against them. First, the National Front was incapable of dealing with the increasing communism waves, and second, the absolute suppression of communist peasants and labour movements was in contradiction with the declared approach of Mosaddeq and his advocators, through which they had come to power. The reformists were again doubtful whether the country could survive in this chaos, and they were willing to maintain the social order. Look no further than the letters of Taqizadeh, a leading constitutionalist, to some cabinet members, in one of which he wrote: 'the country may survive under an unjust and coercive ruler, but will certainly fall as a result of … extremism in freedom,' since according to him, 'poor state officials constantly have to respond to criticism and defamation, (and) then nothing will stand' (Katouzian, 2009: 238). From this viewpoint, the 1953 coup was rather against the labour movement and more specifically the Tudeh Party. For this reason, it benefitted mostly from the support of high-ranking clerics such as Kashani and Borujerdi. The coup first gave the monarchy the means of religion as a powerful weapon, which could be used as an effective tool against the leftist movements, and second, provided the religious bourgeoisie and clerics with golden historical opportunities that later paved the way for them.

This strategy was completed by the Land Reforms, which commenced in the early 1950s. This policy, nonetheless, required establishing a police dictatorship and suppressing all fronts including the opposition factions and parties. For instance, negotiations between Prime Minister Amini and the National Front to implement this policy ultimately failed (Amini, 1997). This was because implementing such a plan in a society like Iran was impossible without the existence of a suppressive bureaucratic political and military force. Thus, the National Front's parties attempting to return to the political scene in the 1960s stepped aside from their political activities due to the increasing suppression. Also, the Tudeh Party, following the

1953 coup, could no longer be publicly active by any means. Nonetheless, later political and social changes gave another chance to the middle faction. Part of the reformists, such as Shapour Bakhtiar and Mozzafar Baghai, reached their desires in the 1970s, however, with a different facet compared to that of the past, although they were not backed by the majority of the reformists. Reformism's orientation towards religion in this period had two main reasons, first, because the regime and its intelligence service, Savak, would suppress any kind of leftist movement, and second, due to the reason that religiosity or religion-oriented reformism could fight communism and labour movements. It is unsurprising then that reformism in this period further incorporated religious features. This led to the emergence of a fascist police-state where the leftists were purged and the state gave room to the clergy that provided the ground for the 1979 Revolution.

Reformism as a movement, especially after the Land Reform, was different from the reformism that the regime itself embarked on. The reformist movement implies the tendencies and orientations of the competing factions. Following the White Revolution and the events of June, both in 1963, the streams of the middle faction attempted to cover their demands with an ideological cloth. They, including Mehdi Bazargan, Ezzatollah Sahabi, and Ali Shariati sought to reconcile Islam and science. Such streams formed a unit faction by way of adapting religion to modern science and affairs, reconciling such beliefs with Western thoughts regarding political, legal, civil, and cultural order (Ganji & Moheimany, 2021: 138). Generally, they were attempting to enter the political structure and gain more privileges by employing a legitimate mechanism that the Shah had founded. Nonetheless, focusing on the religious identity of the new regime is misleading, since, during the revolution, the government changing merely its external appearance maintained the social order. While the Shah was overthrown, the state was not dismantled (Abrahamian, 2008).

## From Revolution to Revolutionary Reformism (1979–1997)

The economic crisis in the mid-1970s and the special position of Iran in the strategy of the US towards the Middle East was finding a solution for saving the country from political collapse and the danger of labour movements and strikes. The solution was creating an open political environment, although the Shah did not consider such protests a real challenge. In this situation, part of the reformists, especially secular nationalists and liberalists, desired a positional power, however low, and a tribute for expressing their political, social, civil thoughts. Nonetheless, reformism was no longer a solution to put an end to the crisis, considering the dictatorship and absolute domination. Unlike the 1963 demonstrations, the regime was confronted by opposition from both secular nationalists and religious leaders in the late 1970s (Moens, 1991).

On the other hand, the lower faction that from the Constitutional Revolution to the 1979 Revolution was seeking the privilege of being in the political structure but had been widely suppressed, also allied with the middle faction a few years before the revolution. The liberal reformism stream was unable to move onto the power structure and find a solution to exit from the crisis; it also lacked enough bases, organisation, networks, or a massive influence on the masses. Its intended government and the rule of law faded amid the widespread protests and social riots. On the flip side, however, the religion-oriented stream had aimed to dominate the political power structure to consolidate its dominance of all social aspects and political areas since the Constitutional Revolution. It had every means, including wide networks with social influence, associations, money (e.g., endowments, the regime's financial support), support of the liberal reformists, and most importantly, support of the masses. Hence, this stream no longer felt the need for reformism in the existing framework of the monarchy.

Nonetheless, since the political order had collapsed and reconstruction of the new government required the presence of the reformists in the political structure, the system which was raised from the 1979 Revolution, at least from its transition period to consolidation period, needed a coalition between liberal reformists and the religion-based faction. However, the revolutionary situation did not allow the continuance of the presence of liberal reformists in power later. The reasons for this were that first, the liberal reformists lacked the ability and strength to suppress or were not suppressive enough to face the challenges in different regions of Iran, and second, factions that contributed to the formation of the new regime were highly divided. Religious forces were willing to establish a political and legal order which was impossible without eliminating their opponents such as leftists, women activists, seculars, nationalists, and supporters of the West.

A new reform era was initiated in 1997 when the Rafsanjani's government (1989–1997) was unable to reconstruct the remains of the wartime, the regime was facing disruption of the circle of capital generation of Iran, and the system was in danger of collapse of the Iranian capitalism due to widespread riots of the marginalised people in many cities. Likewise, the regime failed to deal with the constant high inflation and had a dark record in terms of human rights. In this situation, the very forces that were the real founders of the regime, and had tied their identity with revolutionary actions at the outset of the revolution by opposing the West and especially the US, in the new era, emerged as the pioneers of reform. It was they who raised the flag of reformism again, for saving the circle of production of capitalism from collapse, and most importantly, eliminating the threat of increasing social dissatisfactions, protests, and riots. While promoting concepts such as dialogue of civilisations, religious democracy (*Mardom Salari Dini*), civil society, freedom of speech, and interaction with the West, they attempted to guarantee the survival of the political regime. But the main paradox for the new reformists was that their power was limited to executive and bureaucratic branches of the government, they attempted to seize some aspects of the core pillar of the sovereignty power.

Nevertheless, they lacked the capacity and enough power to respond to social demands in the long run. Also, reformism could lead to the re-emergence of those expectations that existed amid the revolution or the solidification period of the regime (first years after the revolution) but were massively suppressed by the rulers. Once again, reformism was theorised by moderate Islamic thinkers such as Abdolkarim Soroush under religious intellectualism. All these attempts can be considered superficial since the legacy of reformism was soon ruined by the establishment that was no longer in danger politically, and neither did it need economic reconstruction. Ultimately, the repressive policies of the regime put an end to reformism and paved the way for the conservatives. Reformism was a temporary solution, and in the Khatami period (1997–2005), the same dissatisfactions emerged. In other words, reformism, instead of being a step towards responding to the economic, cultural, and political demands of the different social layers, result-wise, is rather a ground builder of a situation where any possibility of advancing such aims through strengthening military and authoritarian forces is postponed. It leads to strengthening forces that put off the agenda the ideas that they had proposed.

## Conclusion

Reformism in Iran has been a struggle between different factions within the bourgeoisie class rather than a class conflict. The bourgeoisie of Iran has historically had religious characteristics. For instance, most streams even in the lower faction, from Babism to People's Mojahedin, had a religious characteristic (Keddie, 1962: 268). The reason why reformism is religious is not merely related to the historical thoughts and ideologies tied with it. Even different social peasant movements in history had shown themselves to the masses with religious identity in their fight with feudal rulers to gain support from people. Simply put, opposition factions have no weapon better than religion. Thus, the most religious forces among different factions were in the frontlines of almost all social and labour movements.

Reformism is highly unlikely to take place in Iran because the country is institutionally and economically incapable of responding to the demands of the masses. Thus, it is rather imposed as a top-down model on the masses and not vice versa. In other words, it is a solution to exit out of the crisis when the government is lacking popularity or legitimacy or is in need. Iranian capitalism under the current historical conditions, and for guaranteeing its survival at least in the mid-term. Likewise, the regime needs a specific type of planning for labour and production, controlling the country, putting pressure on people domestically, and diplomacy or a foreign policy of conflict or struggling internationally.

The complete and organic composition of capital and private ownership, maintaining political and economic order, controlling through military and other institutions, running ideological institutions, holding the power of nationalist mobilisation, conflicting with the US policies in the Middle East, and the existing expansionism in the region are all necessary for the regime. These are the main features of the strategy of the survival of the political system. In a situation where the political, economic, legal, civil, and social aspects of life get the form of militaristic and ideologic, and the power structure gets an oligarchic form, reformism is not a determining factor in the long-time strategy of the regime.

Being a part of the bourgeoisie class of Iran, reformist movements have often sought political and economic changes for the survival of the sovereignty of capitalism. Nonetheless, when state institutions and structures take a political, bureaucratic, and militaristic shape to guarantee the survival of sovereignty, reformism is overlooked in policy-making and planning, although it needs to be in power if it wants to have a social presence and survive.

## References

Abdolamin, M. (2019). *Letters to Nasser al-Din Shah: A collection of petitions containing the Shah's orders to Amin al-Satan, between 1303–1300 AH*. Collection of Literary and Historical Publications of Mahood Afshar Endowment Foundation.

Abrahamian, E. (1968). The crowd in Iranian politics 1905–1953. *Past & Present*, *41*(1), 184–210.

Abrahamian, E. (1979). The causes of the constitutional revolution in Iran. *International Journal of Middle East Studies*, *10*(3), 381–414.

Abrahamian, E. (2008). *A history of modern Iran*. Cambridge University Press.

Amini, A. (1997). *Memoirs of Ali Amini*. H. Ladjevardi, Ed. Goftar.

Ashraf, A. (1980). *Historical obstacles to the growth of capitalism in Qajar Iran*. Zamineh.

Enayat, H. (2013). *Law, state, and society in modern Iran: Constitutionalism, autocracy, and legal reform, 1906–1941*. Palgrave Macmillan.

Foran, J. (1993). *Fragile resistance: Social transformation in Iran from 1500 to the revolution*. Westview Press.

Ganji, N., & Moheimany, M. (2021). The resilient political opportunity structure of Iran. In M. Moheimany (Ed.), *NGOs, policy networks and political opportunities in hybrid regimes*. Palgrave Macmillan.

Ganz, N. (2010). Leading change: Leadership, organization, and social movements. In N. Nohira & R. Kharana (Eds.), *Handbook of leadership: Theory and practice* (pp. 507–526). Harvard Business School.

Ghaffary, G. R., & Azizimehr, K. (2015). Government, civil society and welfare policies in modern Iran. *Journal of Social Science for Policy Implications*, 3(2), 63–82.

Katouzian, H. (2009). *The persians: Ancient, mediaeval and modern Iran*. Yale University Press.

Katouzian, H. (2021). The revolution for law: A chronographic analysis of the constitutional revolution of Iran. *International Journal of Economics and Politics*, 2(1), 63–96.

Keddie, N. (1962). Religion and irreligion in early Iranian nationalism. *Comparative Studies in Society and History*, 4(3), 265–295.

Keddie, N. (1966). *Religion and rebellion in Iran: The Iranian tobacco protest of 1891–1982*. Routledge.

Marx, K., & Engels, F. (1968). *Selected works*. International Publishers.

Moens, A. (1991). President Carter's advisers and the fall of the Shah. *Political Science Quarterly*, 106(2), 211–237.

Morris, A. D., & Staggenborg, S. (2004). Leadership in social movements. In D. A. Snow, S. A. Soule, & H. Kriesi (Eds.), *The Blackwell companion to social movements* (pp. 171–196). Blackwell Publishing.

Poulantzas, N. A. (1973). *Political power and social classes*. NLB; Sheed and Ward.

# 8 The Formation of a Municipal 'Third Sector' in Brazil

*Cícero Augusto Silveira Braga,*
*Mucio Tosta Gonçalves, Thiago Periard*

## Introduction

It has become common to describe contemporary capitalist economies in three 'sectors': the first sector corresponds to that in which the origin and allocation of resources are public and correspond to state actions; the second one concerns the private capitalist enterprise, which aims for profit, in the 'market'; and the third sector is constituted by private, voluntary, non-profitable initiatives which are consolidated in the sphere of non-state public action (Montaño, 2002; Hart et al., 2010).

By third sector is understood a broad set of different institutions that assume legal and political forms of non-governmental organisations (NGOs), foundations and business institutes, community associations, welfare, charitable and philanthropic entities, volunteering, non-profit organisations, public interest organisations or tax exempt, social enterprise, or social economy, among others (Fernandes, 1994; Wango, 2004; Anheier, 2005).

In the Brazilian case, although they have emerged with a welfare character, the first organisations of civil society carried a political cut, as well as different social movements, seeking to promote the empowerment of historically excluded sectors of society, especially in the context of military dictatorship – which seemed to make essential to such organisations the articulation and political organisation of civil society to face the discretionary state (Barbosa, 2006).

The expansion of the third sector in Brazil is considerable: between 1970 and 2016, the number of organisations grew more than 430%, employing almost three million people. There is an expressive segment of those organisations with religious, development, and defence of right objectives. The expansion in the number of these organisations has been greater since the 1980s, because of the adoption of neoliberal-cut economic policies, which, among other effects, reduced the scope of action of pre-existing social welfare policies (Lopez, 2018).

DOI: 10.4324/9781003288145-8

Falconer and Salamon (1998) had argued that the third sector grew as a result of a combination of social and technological changes and the crisis of confidence in the state's capacity. Its expansion resulted from pressures of spontaneous popular movements as well as from public and private organisations and institutions. At the same time, it was also the result of the crises combined effects of the modern welfare state, real socialism, and the economic and environmental model of development adopted in the country from the 1950s onwards.

For Kaloudis (2017), the non-governmental organisations were once identified as providers of assistance and charity services. According to the same author, however, they have expanded their roles to include promoting economic and social development, representing and defending interests through formal legal means, agenda setting, providing public education, monitoring international treaties, etc.

Fernandes (1994) argues that third sector organisations guide their strategies by self-organisation, independence, and plurality, besides being proliferating and politically directed to citizenship and autonomy that compose their base and non-philanthropic groups.

Barbosa (2006) describes some additional functions as the most important ones for the third sector and its organisations: the construction of a nation project; expansion of democracy through citizen formation and strengthening of democratic culture among individuals, strengthening the identity and equal participation; and reconstitutionalisation of the public dimension of society.

In relation to the sectors' agents and purposes, the third sector is, in short, a set of organisations and private initiatives that aim to produce public goods and services. This definition avoids the interpretation limitations of mainstream economic theory, by which such goods and services are perceived only as those that are provided by the government due to the existence of market failures – without discussing whether and why markets fail, and what the alternatives are in terms of regulating them (Meirelles, 2010).

According to Olak (1999), the interests and particular management actions of these types of organisations should submit to the common community interests, since their goals are linked to the production of social change and their resources, including assets, should be used to meet these goals, without distribution among providers.

For Witesman (2016), although the legal and operational definitions of third-sector non-profit organisations are the most usual, they do not account for understanding the institutional nature of such organisations. According to this author, the development of organisational forms in the three sectors has generated a 'blurring' of the boundaries between them, either because the social objectives of the state, private companies, and third sector organisations may converge in the same direction, or because some models for obtaining funds from non-profit organisations 'tie' them to governments, among other reasons.

Such a situation suggests that the use of non-governmental and non-profit categories, if done on the basis of a legalistic definition, is simplifying. Witesman (2016) further argues that one should use an institutional theory which understands that sectors are more 'parallel' than hierarchical and that distinguishes public and private organisations by taking into consideration: '(a) the voluntary (rather than coercive) assignment of roles and (b) the use of the good or service by non-payers' (Witesman, 2016: 97S).

In the definition of the third sector, the functionality and efficiency of organisations that operate under its logic depend on the role and the relations that they maintain with a strategic public formed by person(s) and/or group(s) that perform(s) some investment or have investment interests in them – that is, the stakeholders (Fowler, 2013).

Buček and Smith (2000), addressing European cases, and Bresser-Pereira and Grau (1998), regarding Brazil, argue that the third sector is a space of participatory formalisation or direct democracy, making possible citizen participation in public affairs, which even generates the possibility of joint production of public goods. Pestoff (2008) argues that such organisations have a democratic potential by allowing the creation of new participative channels and influence of citizenship on the state apparatus – even if they are not institutionalised and formalised or even recognised by political science.

Grohs (2021) argues that, despite creating rights and modifying 'corporatist' modes of articulation and interpenetration between the public and private sectors, the participation of the third sector in the joint production of public goods with the state presents several obstacles and asymmetries, which may undermine the potential legitimacy and effectiveness of this type of arrangement.

Moreover, for Montaño (2002), the term 'third sector' is not neutral, due to the fact that it carries a provenance and functionality with the interests of a specific class, since it was coined by organic intellectuals of capital. The author points out that the term has three diversities: one theoretical; other associated with the definition of agents that make up the third sector; and yet another related to the character of the sector itself. Thus, if the third sector reflects the identity of actions produced by civil society, and institutions (state, market, etc.) are constructed by society, the third sector should be, in fact, the first sector.

For Montaño (2002), the sector includes a range of actors that, despite trying to establish themselves as a specific sector of society, seem to be more a mixture of subjects that identify themselves as to certain objectives, strategies, and activities of social promotion, at the same time that they have diverse interests, spaces, and social meanings – sometimes contrary and sometimes even contradictory among themselves.

The discussion proposed by Montaño (2002) allows us to evaluate whether the definitions of third sector organisations should be those of 'non-governmental,' 'self-governed,' and 'non-profit.' That is why these definitions are contradictory: for example, it is impossible to combine the non-governmental nature of an organisation with the nature of a formal 'partner' of the state, or the nature of an agent to meet specific demands, including those of large companies, with 'self-governance.'

Despite this debate about the nature and functions of third sector organisations, there is a consensus in the literature that there is a figure or group that assumes leadership roles in them. There is no consensus, however, about the attributions, characteristics, and distinctions of these leadership figures in different organisations (MacMillan & McLaren, 2012).

In a broad literature review, Hodges and Howieson (2017) show that leadership in the third sector is based in several positions and roles such as governance, strategising, managing human resources, among others. These different approaches must be analysed by each organisation and should consider the leadership model (with theories and ideas of leading process and improvement), leadership philosophy (that dictates the values-based ideas of how the leader will act), and the leadership style, that classifies and describes their behaviour (Howieson & Hodges, 2014). In this work, we address these issues by providing insights through the organisation we are studying and a brief literature review on the empirical evidence.

Green (2009) pointed out that in addition to budgetary, political, and regulatory issues, among other problems, the lack of leadership can be indicated as one of the five main constraints that the third sector encounters, which makes the topic one of special importance for the understanding and strengthening of these organisations.

Among the evidence found, it is very common that leadership appears more as an 'approach,' and not as a defined and stipulated role. According to Hodges and Howieson (2017), the characteristics that define a leader in the organisation they have researched, in the UK, are mainly those of maintaining the organisation's reputation, ensuring ethical obligations and people's motivation, creating a positive environment and collaborative relationships, as well as maintaining innovation, distinction, and enhancing the legitimacy of the third sector.

For Nascimento (2012), according to the responses of participants in a survey in Portugal, the effective leader must hold the following characteristics: 'motivate employees,' 'have a vision,' 'relate respectfully with subordinates,' and 'resolve conflicts.' In addition, Cruz et al. (2014) scored the following qualities as being fundamental for a leader of third sector organisations: planning and setting objectives, organisation and coordination, command and decision, control, delegation, conflict management, initiative, creativity, critical spirit, and the formulation of quantifiable goals.

The field of leadership role in the third sector still lacks further studies. In a broad systematic review, Nascimento (2014) suggests that studies on this sector are approached by overly broad concepts that are not able to faithfully explain its specificities, especially in Southern countries. In fact, most of the evidence on leadership in the third sector focuses on organisations located in countries of the Global North, which have common organisational structures and legislation.

This cutout is problematic since, as pointed out, third sector organisations are born precisely to supply demands that are not adequately offered by governments and/or the market. Expanding the observation on the theme, even if from a specific point of view, will allow us to capture the interrelationships existing in the organisations. This is because, as Hopkins (2010) stated

> good leadership is vital given the complex and dynamic third sector environment. While many of the qualities required of leaders in the third sector are similar to those leading in other sectors, there are distinct skills and behaviors needed to be successful in the sector as a result of its multiple stakeholder relationships and challenges that are qualitatively different from the public and private sectors.
>
> (Hopkins, 2010: 26)

To debate the leadership(s) role(s) of this kind of organisation as a driving force for their continuity and expansion, we discussed the case of a third sector organisation, a non-profit institute. Namely, the *Instituto Miguel Fernandes Torres* is analysed in this chapter, which is an organisation based in the municipality of Ouro Branco, Minas Gerais.

## The Institute: Organisation and Continuity of a Third Sector Organisation from the Perspective of its Leaders

The Institute was created in 2002, initially as a 'Project,' called *Vem Ser* (*Come to Be*) Project, to be developed in the scope of the municipality where it operates, after the coordinator and another educator observed a lack of effective pedagogical and educational practices in an existing project implemented at a local school unit, through which sports activities were offered.

When defining what the "Project" was, the responsible for its creation states that

> When I arrived, the children would stay here just playing with a ball, so my idea was that these children would have other activities. There was only the Toriba Project, the one from the state government. And I didn't agree with children just playing with a ball for four hours. So, me and another person, who started with me, *the educator*, we started preparing children, doing homework with them, studying for tests with them, we brought things from home to make handicrafts with them. We did it on our own. (...) we had no resources. (...) When we started, we had nothing, not even chairs for the children to sit on, we had nothing inside here and, little by little, with all the donations, we were getting other things, according to what children wanted.
> (verbal recorded statement given in an interview held on 26/10/2015)

The initiative to which the interviewee referred to is the *Esporte Solidário Toriba* programme, which was developed by the State Secretariat of Sports of the Minas Gerais state government between 1997 and 2000.

Considering the difficulties in making permanent the actions that she was trying to initiate through *Vem Ser* Project, the person responsible for the idea of its implementation and the organisation of the first actions of the 'Project' was oriented to register it as a legal entity, so that she could raise funds and, therefore, operationalise the project more effectively. Until then, the 'Project' counted on only two employees (who are also its founders), who had to ensure the functioning of activities, working as teachers, conducting crafts and sports workshops, among other activities (Braga, 2015).

In this sense, according to the statement given by *the educator*, she started working in the organisation as the workshop supervisor and administrator. This implied that she had to 'go to schools, seek students, find supplies and everything' (recorded verbal statement given in an interview held on 26/10/2015).

Besides the problem with the staff, the 'Project' faced problems such as lack of minimal inputs for the development of activities. Still as narrated the educator:

> we had nothing, practically nothing. I worked with the straw workshop; we had no chair to sit on for children to work. The children worked standing up. There were no stools in the cafeteria, they also ate standing

up. And, in the living room, we didn't even have a table. They used an iron frame structure, with an old door on top, for us to work with.

(verbal recorded statement given in an interview held on 26/10/2015)

The beginning of the 'Project' was marked by political conflicts, which required the project coordinator to impose herself to ensure its establishment in the city. To this end, the coordinator reported that when she envisioned the 'Project,' she considered it important that the organisation was to be run fundamentally like a business, even if the goal was not to generate profits. Thus, the leadership role assumed by her can be initially identified as being the search for the institutional formalisation of the 'Project,' as well as the search for partnerships.

The first result of the manager's actions was harvested on 2 September, in 2002, when the reports of the General Assembly meeting were signed for the creation and approval of the Social Statute and the election and inauguration of members from the Board of Directors and the Fiscal Council of the Association of the then 'Project,' which was formally identified as *Instituto Criança*.

The statute of this new non-profit civil society defined its objectives, in its first article, as follows:

> a) To represent and defend the interests of its members, composed of children, adolescents and youth of low income, with public and private institutions, or wherever it is necessary, aiming to sign agreements or contracts of any nature, for their benefit, especially with regard to obtaining transportation, food, educational supplies, sponsorships for sports, educational and recreational activities, leisure, arts, culture, dance, tourism or other related activities; c) To act as co-responsible, with SEESP - Secretaria de Estado de Esportes de Minas Gerais, to make feasible the operationalization of Esporte Solidário Project (...); d) Promote events and cultural activities; e) Organize events, festivals, raffles, among others, aiming at financial resources.

(*Vem Ser* Project, 2002)

In 2005, the Institute established a partnership with the City Hall, which provided employees to work in the new organisation. Soon after, it also started to count on the work of volunteers. In addition, it was registered with the Municipal Council for Children and Adolescents (Conselho Municipal da Criança e do Adolescente – CMDCA) and with the Municipal Council for obtaining registration as a public utility organisation within the scope of the municipality.

With these formalisations, the support of a large multinational company from the mining and steel sector, based in the municipality, was obtained, as well as the support of local business organisations, initially through the donation of supplies to guarantee the entity's operation.

The Institute was born in a context of voluntary action, from the merger of projects of governmental interest and in a moment of impulse for the creation of civil society organisations in the country. But it was not the first organisation of its kind in the city.

The distribution of civil society organisations in the city, by area of activity, indicates that 37% had as their main activity the development and defense of rights, 22% were religious, 20% acted in the field of culture and recreation, and 4.9% aimed at social assistance (Ipea, 2019).

Specifically, the Institute presents itself, in its blog, in a news item dated 15 March 2009, as a civil society organisation of public interest, but still using the fantasy name 'Project.' Its objectives, as described in this blog, which has been 'offline' since 2015, were the following:

> it carries out social assistance actions aimed at the public between 7 and 18 years of age, with the objective of helping children and adolescents in situations of social vulnerability, offering them care and food services, workshops, sports, and school reinforcement, the latter aiming to encourage students to stay in school, the reintegration to the learning process and the reduction of the school failure rate through the guidance of the coordinator and constant exchange between the Institute and schools where they are enrolled, as well as other aspects that may arise which are seen as necessary for the cognitive, psychomotor, affective, and social growth and development of these youngsters in formation.

In 2015, through its Action Plan, the Institute defined that its purposes were to assist and socially promote children, adolescents, adults, and families, in order to promote the social and personal development of these subjects.

The same document maintains the emphasis on the priority assistance to children, adolescents, and youngsters from seven to 18 years old, domiciled in Ouro Branco, in its urban perimeter or in rural areas. The service should be provided by offering pedagogical support and developing sports activities, as well as workshops on decoupage, cloth art, computers, musical instruments, and chess.

Besides this public, the Institute also attended people indicated by the Reference Center for Social Assistance – CRA and by the Specialized Center for Reference in Social Assistance – Creas, in sewing workshops and other labour activities.

According to Prosas electronic platform, which discloses information and data on the selection and monitoring of social projects (https://prosas.com.br/sobre, accessed on 1 October 2019), the Child Institute aims to serve children and adolescents between seven and 17 years of age, in the afterschool period (morning and afternoon), from Mondays to Fridays, who are regularly enrolled in the municipal network and have characteristics that fit them primarily into conditions of social vulnerability. According to the same source, in 2018, 330 vacancies were offered for this public, a number that varies over time depending on the resources raised by the NGO.

The assistance to children aims to 'contribute to school performance and flow through the construction of the individual.' This goal is justified because the maintenance of school flow is an important educational challenge, since, despite being enrolled, students' progress every year with large gaps between age, grade, and in content belonging (according to https://prosas.com.br/, accessed on 1 October 2019).

Among the documents mentioned dated 2009 (electronic), 2015 (Action Plan) and 2019, it was possible to identify two perceptible changes in relation to the definition that the Institute makes of its own 'identity': the first is the denomination as a Civil Society Organisation of Public Interest. The second refers to the goal of serving children and adolescents in situations of social vulnerability.

In the first case, it may be simply an information error, perhaps due to the fact that the person responsible for creating the blog got confused. As the blog did not continue after the date previously mentioned, it is not known for sure what – and why – this occurred.

Considering that the definitions of third sector organisations point to them as actors in a public space, the absence of clear communication strategies for the Institute indicates limitations to its participation in important local and supra-local dialogues. To some extent, this is a result of both material difficulties of the organisation, and the inexistence of a sufficiently strong network that has allowed it to sustain greater capacities to vocalise demands and ideas.

In any case, it is an important indication to think about the degree of informality with which a formalised organisation deals with a crucial legal issue. Even because in consultation with the Ministry of Justice portal that registers Oscip in the country, only four registrations of this type of entity were found in the municipality where *Instituto Criança* is located, and it was not among them (available at http:// portal.mj.gov.br/SistemaOscip/resultadoconsulta.asp, accessed on 29 June 2021).

Furthermore, the Institute's managers have made efforts to circumvent this type of problem, by creating profiles, increasing the number of posts on social networks, and adopting more effective virtual communication strategies. This change is marked especially by some key events. The first of them is related to the restrictions imposed by the public health emergency situation caused by the new coronavirus pandemic, which required adapting the teaching methodologies to a remote modality. In addition, the coordinator started a course with *Falcons University* on management and dissemination of social projects.

This change in the way of acting by communication is related to a central event for the discussion of the Institute organisation as a third sector entity relating to the generational aspect: the Institute started to count on the advice of two young professionals, who have greater mastery of virtual strategies and techniques of communication. This theme is relevant because it allows us to think about a prejudice commonly associated with the universe of organisations managed by the elderly, that of ageism. In general terms, the issue is that youth is perceived as being adapted to new information technologies and, therefore, more productive. What was noticed in the case of the Institute is that the prejudice does not exist, but the idea that young women are more 'capable,' which crossed many opinions expressed by the coordinator in her last interview, allowed us to identify that this type of problem exists.

The second change made by the Institute regarding the definition of its nature, between 2009 and 2015, was the definition of its target audience. In the case of the use of vulnerability idea, although certainly applicable to poor Brazilian children and youth population, it requires precision as to its use, since this idea can be defined as a set of situations and conditions of human life that involve individual dimensions (including biological), economic, social, and cultural (delimiting it as a phenomenon in the field of citizenship).

In a first sense, the word indicates the existence of danger or the possibility of damage. As Nichiata et al. (2008) describe, in health research, the term is used to designate the 'susceptibility of people to health problems and harm.' In this sense, it is not distinguished from the concept of risk.

However, there is a distinction between vulnerability and risk, depending on the more or less synthetic nature of the description. That is, while the first term seeks to theoretically associate abstract elements components of physical and social processes, individual and collective, applicable to each and every individual, the idea of risk is probabilistic, or measurable (Cunico & Oka-Fiori, 2014; Schumann, 2014).

Marandola Jr. and Hogan (2005) argue that the analysis of vulnerability began to refer to the existing relations between population and development in community, family, and individual levels. From then on, emphasis has been given to the notion of vulnerable groups. Thus, vulnerability is understood from three components: (1) the existence of a potentially adverse event (risk), endogenous or exogenous; (2) inability to respond to the situation, either because of inefficiency of their defenses or lack of resources that support it; (3) inability to adapt to the situation generated by the materialization of the risk.

(Marandola Jr. and Hogan, 2005: 22)

According to Costa et al. (2018), the growing literature on the subject associates vulnerability and poverty, the former being a symptom, or one of the dimensions or a resultant of the former, by being susceptible to it.

Agreeing with Castel (1997) that individuals are inserted in the world from the 'universes' of work and social relations of proximity, not necessarily labour relations, one can then think that vulnerability is the result of the conjunction of work precariousness with the fragility of relational supports obtained with the family and the community.

The discussion on vulnerability, then, should be associated with issues related to perceptions and social representations of danger and risk, as well as those that refer to resilience – or the ability of a body and/or a system (and, by analytical extension, human social subjects) to absorb changes and impacts that affect it, while maintaining the relationships between the elements that compose it (Teixeira, 2019), recovering from them quickly – which characterises the resilient as someone resistant and flexible (Manyena, 2006).

Such definitions do not allow one to understand the *Instituto Criança* as an entity actually engaged in vulnerability reversal policies. Unless one understands the use of the term in a limited way, representing the common expression of the idea of risk.

In any case, the Institute seems to wish to organise itself to act in a broader territory than the municipal one, where it is installed. Thus, for instance, in October of 2009, the Institute became, by request, a member of the Executive Association of Support to Watershed Management Peixe Vivo – *Agência Peixe Vivo* (according to the register available at http://agenciapeixevivo.org.br/wp-content/uploads/2017/10/8.-Ata-1%C2%AA-Assembleia-Geral-Ex.-01-10-09.pdf).

Still in what seemed to be an effort to expand the scope of its actions, the Institute was included in the Municipal Education Plan 2015–2024 of the municipality where it is located, as a partner entity to the *Educação Integral* project proposed by the City Hall.

These partnerships, as the coordinator pointed out, are important, since the Institute's public and private partners 'give us the rod and teach us how to fish, but don't give us the fish. So, we are the ones who have to obtain it.'

Thus, the role of these partnerships is understood by the coordinator as one of the pillars that allows their work to keep improving, even though she ensures that the activities are dialogical and attentive to the targeted audience demands.

In 2021, with a staff of 38 people, 27 of whom are contractors, three are service providers, two are on loan from the City Hall, and five are volunteers, the Institute was assisted by a management company for third sector organisations.

The Institute receives most of its income through an agreement with the Municipal Education Secretariat. In addition to this source, it counts on resources donated by the aforementioned multinational company installed in the municipality through several transference modalities. Among these, the following stand out

- The execution of repair works in its facilities, in 2017 (according to https://vertentesdasgerais.com.br/gerdau-investe-mais-de-r-600-mil-em-projetos-sociais-voltados-educacao-em-2017/).
- A prize in the amount of R$15,000.00 for the development of the 'Water that Feeds' Project, granted for a period of two years.
- A sponsorship from the Project '*Corpo – Educação e Mente*' (*Body – Education and Mind*), in the amount of R$78,379.73, for the period from March to December 2019, counting on resources from the *Fundo da Infância e do Adolescente* (*Childhood and Adolescent Fund*) – FIA, previously mentioned.

Other sources of income for the entity are charitable events, such as those promoted by students from the Federal Institute of Minas Gerais, with a campus in the city, in 2019, in addition to the sale of handmade products made in workshops offered to children and adolescents.

In 2019, the Institute was recognised as a charitable entity with the Certificate of Charitable Entities of Social Assistance – Cebas, in the area of education, which allows it to obtain special tax treatment (with exemptions). The validity of the recognition is in effect until the year 2024.

Given this previously described scenario, the founders were questioned about the role of the 'second sector' in the dynamics and organisation of the entity, since it has significant importance in building it.

Once the Institute started without minimum infrastructure, it was through the partnerships that the creation and continuity of the activities were made possible. These partnerships were built in different ways, for example, through donations of supplies, demand for inputs such as the staff uniforms, minister for lectures, among others. The recognition of this help is very clear in the founders' speech.

Thus, for the educator: 'without this help it is impossible, there is no way. Because City Hall provides some help, but it's not enough. So we end up having to seek other projects, other companies, to be able to maintain the Project.'

In addition, the coordinator comments: 'this is extremely important. Because if we don't have the financial support, what weighs the most for us is the part of employees because of social charges, which we would have to cut.'

The educator adds that the importance of maintaining the 'Project' is a positive answer for the local society in relation to the deficiencies of public policies for the care of children, as follows:

> It is in fact positive. And this is not only for the Project, but for society as a whole. Actually, if we receive this help, we end up helping society as a whole too, because if children come here, parents can work. If they don't come, the parents can't work, because they have to take care of their children, so one thing pulls the other.
> 
> (verbal recorded statement given in an interview made by the author on 26/10/2015)

In this sense, the coordinator reinforces the importance of these donations, since:

> how many times these companies can donate a percentage of their income tax to FIA? If they don't donate to FIA, it goes to the government. The government, nobody here will know what they are doing. And if the company donates, for the very place where it is, it will be able to look, to inspect what we are doing with the money. So, what I think is positive is that, if the company uses things from here, like, for example, Gerdau extracts the ore from here; the amount of people that come here to work, the social difficulties that exist when this amount of people come, especially when there is an apparatus, something like that. If Gerdau contributes here, it is also positive for the town. If it takes things from here, if it takes its profit from here, it has to give a counterpart.
> 
> (verbal recorded statement given in an interview made by the author on 26/10/2015)

It should be noted that, for the coordinator, these partnerships are essential not only for budgetary purposes, but also for the legitimisation of the Institute with the external public, whether society or specific interest institutions. For the coordinator, the Institute's image associated with renowned names from the second sector, as is the case of the multinational company, caused the municipal government to see them differently because 'they had a renowned company as a reference.'

However, both have as a perspective the possibility of being self-sufficient and no longer needing to submit to either the market or the state. The coordinator, in a first moment, stated that her wish was that: 'our ideal is to be highly sustainable. Because one of our biggest difficulties is financial resources, actually. The ideal would be for us to be able to stand on our own. So, whatever comes is profit' (recorded verbal statement given during interview by the author on 26/10/2015).

The role that the Institute attributes to the support it receives should also be highlighted. It was pointed out by interviewees that, if the financial resources received from the City Hall are assured, those coming from companies are not. However, this second source seems to be better received than the first, once the autonomy to manage the resources that come from it is greater. This is a crucial aspect of the question discussed in this chapter: what is the meaning of social inclusion actions for vulnerable people when third sector organisations see the state as an actor that must provide funding, while companies take the role of benefactors?

Managers of the Institute have a critical perception about the dependence on these resources, since they seem to know that they represent the use of tax benefits by the main donating company. In addition, they also point out that another reason for such donations is the use of this mechanism as a marketing action, within the scope of so-called corporate social responsibility.

Symbolically, however, the choice of the interviewees' words, in relation to the desired financial autonomy of the 'Project' and the Institute, reveals between the lines that self-sufficiency and the use of 'market' sponsorship are not opposed, which seems to put a limit to a project against vulnerability and of responsibility towards a new society.

In general, all these relations go through the figure of the coordinator, who assumes possible mistakes, but also recognises the necessity of the effort spent individually so that the 'Project' could get to where it is today. She points out that, today, the Institute is the fulfilment of a dream that she describes as follows: 'we started as a grain of sand, but one day we will be sea.' This effort is also recognised by the city's community and bodies with which the Institute relates, who recurrently mention the Institute as the 'coordinator's project.'

This position brings with it a challenge regarding the continuity of the organisation. The coordinator reported that she is officially retired and her work at the Institute, although unchanged, has become voluntary. This is because, as she reports, 'people want jobs and not work' and, therefore, if she hires 'anyone to take care of it, the "Project" ends.'

In this sense, the coordinator has been trying to train new people that can take over the continuity of the Institute, but very carefully, since it is, above all, a personal achievement. Here we have, in another perspective, what was previously mentioned as the problem of ageism, but under another format: the senior's choice for young people who are competent to 'run' the Institute, but not necessarily competing with management.

Nowadays, during the social isolation due to the Covid-19 pandemic, the Institute couldn't be open for children. In this new reality, the alternative was to develop classes remotely, allowing children to remain linked to teaching and learning systems. However, not all children and teenagers had and/or have equipment and/or access to the internet in order to participate and develop activities. In this sense, the Institute created local support points to access the internet and print materials provided by the school, enabling interaction, learning, and prevention of rights violations.

Despite the problems we had perceived about the Institute's leadership capacity, these (not so simple) initiatives related to the offer of support points to children suggest that is possible to build a new chapter in its history.

## Conclusion

Having understood the concept of NGOs, therefore, we come to *Instituto Criança*. The Institute follows, in general terms, the 'recipe' of what is understood as such an organisation. A new entity, it needs to align itself with both the so-called first and second sectors in order to maintain its functionality. The search for autonomy should be, then, the main objective at the moment.

This is because, even with a set of socially relevant actions at the municipal level, expressed through its continuity and the support it receives, the Institute is not an actor aimed at transforming social reality. In this sense, we recover the problematisation made by Montaño (2002), for whom a social transformation project requires objective and subjective conditions, understanding that the intentionality of individuals and groups is not enough, by itself, to create a new society. That said, it is important to understand that social order is the product of a struggle between the subalterns and the class that holds power, using it to manipulate the 'life world.' It is in this space, between the state and private companies, that organisations of the third sector must seek to find their identity, at the risk of being pressed out, becoming a sham solution to socio-environmental problems that afflict contemporary society under the power of capital.

In accordance with this discussion, the particularities of the third sector are not yet well-defined either. This is because, to the extent that the third sector organises itself from its own needs, its functional structure should occur accordingly. In particular, the role of leadership has as many definitions as there are institutions.

In fact, from the observation of the Institute analysed in this work, we see that there was – and there is – the search for some professionalism that can structure the organisation so that it can raise more financial resources and expand its capacity to act. However, we also noticed that, in the first instance, these decisions are taken in a domestic and not in a very strategical way, that is, they depend on the figure of the coordinator, the central manager of the project, from whom the decisions are given as definitive.

The impression generated by the observation of the Institute case was that the leadership is somewhat 'lost' in terms of its objectives. Should it 'improve' the quality of life of poor teenage students through their integration via sports? Or ought it promote the transformation of the conditions in which these young people are inserted in the school system? Or promoting a certain security of access to monetary income, through specific actions in order to generate jobs and income for young people? Or even to insert itself in the 'field' of corporate social responsibility actions, obtaining the financial support to do all – or some of the actions listed here?

It was not possible to get clear answers – and maybe, thinking about third sector organisations such as the Institute, this is the possible answer. These are personal efforts, woven about and weaving social networks, that make the task of developing the organisation a set of tribulations. The problem with this type of leadership is therefore not a lack of will, organisational ambition, or even strategic vision. More likely, it is a result of the fact that it is difficult to plan for the long term without having the short term sorted out.

## References

Anheier, H. K. (2005). *Nonprofit organizations*. Routledge.
Barbosa, L. P. (2006). Significados do Terceiro Setor: de uma nova prática política à despolitização da questão social. *Sociedade e Cultura*, 9(1), 173–186.
Braga, C. A. S. (2015). Mercado e Terceiro Setor: Uma observação através do Instituto Miguel Fernandes Torres [Monografia de Curso, Universidade Federal de São João delRei].
Bresser-Pereira, L. C., & Grau, N. C. (1998). Entre el Estado y mercado: lo público no estatal. In L. C. Bresser-Pereira & N. C. Grau (Eds.), *Lo público no estatal en la reforma del Estado* (pp. 25–56). Paidós.
Buček, J., & Smith, B. (2000). New approaches to local democracy: Direct democracy, participation and the "third sector". *Environment and Planning C: Government and Policy*, 18, 3–16.
Castel, R. (1997). A dinâmica dos processos de marginalização: da vulnerabilidade à "desfiliação". *Caderno CRH*, 10(26), 19–40.

Costa, M. A., dos Santos, M. P. G., Marguti, B., Pirani, N., Pinto, C. V. da S., Curi, R. L. C., Ribeiro, C. C., & Albuquerque, C. G. de (2018). *Vulnerabilidade social no Brasil: conceitos, métodos e primeiros resultados para municípios e regiões metropolitanas brasileiras*. Ipea.

Cruz, S., Pais, C., & Parente, C. (2014). Gestão estratégica, liderança, e cultura nas organizações do terceiro setor. In C. Parente (Ed.), *Empreendedorismo social em Portugal* (pp. 152–158). Universidade do Porto.

Cunico, C., & Oka-Fiori, C. (2014). O estado de normalidade e o estado de exceção diante da importância das categorias de "vulnerabilidade", "risco" e "resiliência". *Caminhos de Geografia, 15*(52), 1–20.

Falconer, A. P., Lucas, A., & Salamon, L. (1998). A emergência do terceiro setor– uma revolução associativa global. *Revista de administração, 33*(1), 5–11.

Fernandes, R. C. (1994). *Privado porém público: o terceiro setor na América Latina*. Relume Dumará.

Fowler, A. (2013). *Striking a balance: A guide to enhancing the effectiveness of non-governmental organisations in international development*. Routledge.

Green, H. (2009). *State of the sector panel survey: Introduction and panel characteristics*. Cabinet Office.

Grohs, S. (2021). Participatory administration and co-production. In S. Kuhlmann, I. Proeller, D. Schimanke, & J. Ziekow (Eds.), *Public administration in Germany* (pp. 311–325). Palgrave Macmillan.

Hart, K., Laville, J.-L., & Cattani, A. D. (2010). *The human economy; a citizen's guide*. Polity Press.

Hodges, J., & Howieson, B. (2017). The challenges of leadership in the third sector. *European Management Journal, 35*(1), 69–77.

Hopkins, L. (2010). *Mapping the third sector: A context for social leadership*. The Work Foundation.

Howieson, B., & Hodges, J. (2014). *Public and third sector leadership: Experience speaks*. Emerald Group Publishing.

Ipea. (2019). *Mapa das Organizações da Sociedade Civil*. Instituto de Pesquisa Econômica Aplicada.

Kaloudis, G. (2017). Non-governmental organizations: Mostly a force for good. *International Journal on World Peace, 34*(1), 81–112.

Lopez, F. G. (2018). *Perfil das organizações da sociedade civil no Brasil*. Ipea.

MacMillan, R., & McLaren, V. (2012). *Third sector leadership: The power of narrative*. Third Sector Research Centre.

Manyena, S. B. (2006). The concept of resilience revisited. *Disasters, 30*(4), 433–450.

Marandola Jr, E., & Hogan, D. J. (2005). Vulnerabilidades e riscos: entre geografia e demografia. *Revista Brasileira de Estudos de População, 22*(1), 29–53.

Meirelles, D. S. (2010). Teorias de mercado e regulação: por que os mercados e o governo falham? *Cadernos EBAPE.BR, 8*(4), 644–660.

Montaño, C. E. (2002). *Terceiro setor e questão social: crítica ao padrão emergente de intervenção social*. Cortez Editora.

Nascimento, C. E. P. do (2012). *Estilos de liderança no terceiro setor e repercussão nos níveis de motivação dos colaboradores* [Tese de Doutorado, Instituto Politécnico de Bragança].

Nascimento, T. T. do (2014). *Proatividade no terceiro setor: relações entre liderança e motivação* [Dissertação de Mestrado, Universidade de Brasília].

Nichiata, L. Y. I., Bertolozzi, M. R., Takahashi, R. F., & Fracolli, L. A. (2008). A utilização do conceito" vulnerabilidade" pela enfermagem. *Revista latino-americana de enfermagem, 16*(5), 923–928.

Olak, P. A. (1999). Conceitos econômicos aplicados à contabilidade de entidades privadas sem fins lucrativos. CongressoBrasileiro de Custos-ABC, Anais.

Pestoff, V. A. (2008). *A democratic architecture for the welfare state*. Routledge.

Schumann, L. R. M. A. (2014). *A multidimensionalidade da construção teórica da vulnerabilidade: análise histórico-conceitual e uma proposta de índice sintético* [Dissertação de Mestrado, Universidade de Brasília].

Teixeira, E. C. (2019). *Resiliência e vulnerabilidade social: uma perspectiva para a educação sociocomunitária da adolescência*. Vozes.

Witesman, E. M. (2016). An institutional theory of the nonprofit: Toll goods and voluntary action. *Nonprofit and Voluntary Sector Quarterly, 45*(4 suppl), 97S–115S.

World Association of Non-Governmental Organizations [WANGO]. (2004). *Code of ethics and conduct for NGOs*. Office of United Nations Affairs.

# 9 Constant Swings
## Women's Rights Movements in the Era of Islamic Republic of Iran

*Mohsen Moheimany and Mahdieh Golroo*

### Introduction

In the political settings of modern authoritarian regimes, the interaction between social movements and the state is complicated, as both sides confront one another with paradoxical characteristics and behaviours. When it comes to women's rights movements, the leaders and groups in some Middle Eastern countries have succeeded in effectively pushing back the patriarchism and changing the status quo; but due to the regime's engineering policies and the dependency of social movements on the state funds, some parts of these movements have also become antiselves forces that curtail self-rights under the flag of women's rights, intentionally or unintentionally, by playing according to the authoritarian rules (Sadeghi, 2009a,2009b; Heydemann, 2010). This paradoxical situation makes the women movements ineffective as they become partly critical against patriarchism but partly loyal to it at the same time. Progressive and retrogressive moves in the area of women's rights are the consequences of this complex paradox. This is evident in the trajectory of the women movement in the Islamic Republic of Iran too.

The public spheres of authoritarian regimes have both democratic and authoritarian capacities and shift between the two over time (Heydemann, 2010; Porta & Diani, 1999). Two concepts from the literature of authoritarianism and social movements, namely 'hybrid regime' and 'political opportunity structure' can answer this complexity. The earlier explains the paradox of coexistence between democracy and authoritarianism in today's regimes and the latter is about the periodical shifts that might happen in a regime's character in terms of dealing with social movements.

The concept of hybrid regimes refers to a system that falls in-between democracy and authoritarianism (Diamond, 2002). In such regimes, although different extents of democratic freedoms and capacities may exist, the concentration of power advantages the rulers with the chance

DOI: 10.4324/9781003288145-9

of undermining the independent social movements and raising loyal ones instead of them (Abdolmohammadi & Cama, 2015; Karl, 1995). Hence, irrespective of regime structure, one should take into account the constitutional recognition and respect for basic freedoms, as well as the opportunity for the rise of genuine and independent social movements. In this area, Wigell (2008) emphasises the essential freedoms, namely freedom of expression, organisation, information, and freedom from discrimination, stating that should these rights of citizens and groups be guaranteed and respected, more opportunities for the rise and action of genuine civil societies and critical movements can be expected. In contrast, authoritarian regimes systematically limit constitutional freedoms and, as a result, engineered movements and closed public spheres are most likely to emerge (Porta & Diani, 1999; Tarrow, 1989). This makes the public sphere and political competitions of such countries complicated and paradoxical. These systems restrict competition between political streams, provide a low level of fairness and restricted liberties for non-governmental actors, and repress the basic rights of the citizens (Hydemann, 2010; Karl, 1995).

The Islamic Republic of Iran, as the case of this chapter, is far away from democracy and freedom, as the international indexes show. In its 2021 index, Freedom House ranks Iran as a 'not free' country. Also, the annual democracy index compiled by the Economist Intelligence Unit labels Iran as an 'authoritarian regime,' while having shown a constant decline in its scores over the years leading to 2021. Nevertheless, the Islamic Republic is not a totally authoritarian regime, and like hybrid regimes, it encompasses several elected institutions, such as president and parliament, as well as a constitutional law that requires public participation in government and necessitates guaranteeing political and civil rights of people, and women to a great extent, although with certain limits (Abdolmohammadi & Cama, 2015). The issue of authoritarianism in this regime is concerned with how the power is practised and how the institutions are exploited by the conservative Islamic elites and military forces. This explains why the regime has been moving towards authoritarianism instead of democracy since its establishment.

Hybrid regimes are also capable of showing contradictory traits and behaviours versus their civil society across different periods. Hence, social movements may face different sets of political constraints and possibilities and threats (Koopman, 1999). The concept of political opportunity structure explains this shift (Eisinger, 1973). Particular factors, including the power rotation between the political elites with competing ideologies, the extent of centralisation of power, the features of the electoral system, the stability of political coalitions, and the configuration of elected and unelected institutions are considerable in this respect (Tarrow, 1989). More particularly, being liberal or conservative in ideology from one point of view, and suppressive or tolerant in traits from another point of view determine the political climate and the atmosphere of the country for social movements (Meyer, 2004; Kitschelt, 1985; Porta & Diani, 1999). This is related to the methods that a regime leader/s and state institutions use to repress, silence, and limit civil society groups and activists. Hard methods such as detaining and jailing activists or repressing protests are the more usual and visible but implanting loyal groups and leaders in the civil society, appropriating laws and rules, and also ideologisation of the practices are the soft methods that help to engineer political competitions (Hydemann, 2010; Liverani, 2008).

In terms of engineering the political processes, leaders take advantage of the resources to implant loyalism in society and curb critical forces. Separating between insider and outsider groups of civil society develops a patron-client system of relationships (Lemarchand, 1972). Insiders are the legitimate groups and leaders that benefit from recognition, security, resources, and rewards, as well as inclusion in political processes (Grant, 1989). In the opposite, outsiders either do not seek involvement in policy processes by their own choice or are deprived of formal recognition, resources, and policy consultation by the power holders (Grant, 1989). Discrimination between insiders and outsiders by a regime not only determines the balance of power between social and political forces in the public spheres but also ascertains their position and successes in achieving their rights and demands.

The following sections discuss the trajectory of the women's rights movement in the Islamic Republic era by accounting for the hybrid regime structure and the shifts of tolerance of the regime versus women's rights groups and leaders.

## The Tale of a Rise and a Fall

In Iran, the earliest moves to let women out of house and housekeeping roles were taken when the Qajar Dynasty (1974–1925) implemented westernisation schemes. As a part of state-run reforms, dozens of women from elite families were sent to the European countries for pursuing higher education. They returned to Iran with some intellectual knowledge, especially about democracy and the rule of law. This acquaintance with democracy became a motto for the educated women to take part in the first democratic revolution in Iran, called the Constitutional Revolution (1905) when women appeared alongside men to fight oppression. Later during the rule of the Pahlavi dynasty (1925–1979), further state-initiated reforms provided women with more civil rights and legal achievements such as studying at university and abolition of polygamy, although the government system remained patriarchal (Abbasi, 2014). The reform plans of the Pahlavi kingdom laid the foundations for pursuing new aspirations in the following decades, as women social groups broadened the focus of their activism from the sake of democracy to include women's own status.

The 1979 Islamic Revolution, as the second step towards democratisation in a century, became possible also because of the significant contribution of female students and women activists, and after that, a new generation of women activists went through associationism and activism periods (Namazi, 2000). However, the Islamic Republic unexpectedly and very soon turned out to be the monopoly of a fundamentalist class of clergy that promoted ideological shifts in the political regime. Thus, the revolution did succeed in eliminating the patriarchal authoritarianism of the Pahlavi's regime.

Despite the democratic slogans of the leaders, not only did the new system not bring political or social progress for women but it also made their situation worse. Through establishing numerous patron institutions, including Islamic foundations and organisations, as well as many security and militia forces with an Islamic discourse that had no room for feminist or equalitarian demands, clerics expanded totalitarianism (Abdolmohammadi & Cama, 2015; Sedghi, 2007, Mogheisi, 1991). Khomeini, the architect of the Islamic regime during 1979–1989, mandated a traditional guideline that for women it stressed the notion of 'motherhood' as the key role. Besides that, chastity – meaning not mixing with the opposite sex and protection in society, and modesty – meaning not being vogue to the Islamic rules – were located at the centre of this discourse (Sadeghi, 2009a, 2009b). The two concepts have become institutionalised strongly in the laws and policies during the last four decades. Nevertheless, some limited democratic elements have also been incorporated in the regime's ideology by Khomeini and his successor Khamenei (1989–), as both reluctantly admitted to the importance of women's social role and presence in the political positions (Saeedzade, 1998).

This fundamentalist discourse soon targeted the rules related to women in the bodies of family and criminal laws. In August 1983, the parliament passed the Criminal Laws with several controversial articles, one of which is 'women who appear in public without an Islamic dressing will be sentenced to up to 74 lashes,'; this meant justification of the use of violence against them. These shifts were faced with the street protests of women's rights defenders promptly, especially by the secular and progressive, educated women leaders. Just a few weeks after the Revolution, on 8 March 1979, the International Women's Day, dozens of women in Tehran held a massive rally on the central streets and chanted for their freedom of dress and against mandatory Hijab. Those protests faced crackdown and repression, a reaction that opened the way for future repression of vocal women activists.

Women did not give up but the start of the eight-year war with Iraq from 1981, and the need for national unity, as well as the regime's seeking consolidation, became justifications for the revolutionary state and its loyal forces to isolate gender issues and ignore women's political participation until the mid-1990s (Namazi, 2000). In this period, women were prescribed with a role model of 'good wife' for warriors or their participation was officially defined as supporting Iran's front in the war for supplying ancillary services. The 'external threat' was also used as an excuse to securitise the national atmosphere with the detention and execution of rebellious women activists and female political prisoners, and the ones who used to hold ministerial and parliamentarian posts before the revolution. In the following decades, two political shifts through presidential elections, though still under one fundamentalist leader Ayatollah Khamenei, brought about two opposite periods for the Iranian women movement.

The 1997 presidential elections became a window of opportunity for the young generation of educated women who looked for appealing new rights. More than 40% of women voters voted for a moderate camp that had promoted a political reform plan and nominated Khatami, who had a manifest for enhancing women's rights and status (Gheissari & Nasr, 2006; Tazmini, 2013). During the so-called reformist administration, until 2005, the regime allowed some liberalisations by letting women promote associationism, gain political posts at the state cabinet and city councils, plus a limited number of parliamentary seats, albeit very gradually and with no chance for gaining high-ranking posts like ministries. The reformist administration allocated some funds to the non-state organisations of women, the number of which increased by more than five times according to the centre for women participation (2001, p. 32). These changes further grew the number of women activists and escalated their expectations that were inspired by global feminism, an NGO activist said in a personal interview. By the pressure of feminist NGOs, the reformists in Parliament also passed a bill requiring the government to join the Committee on the Elimination of Discrimination Against Women, an action that however was blocked by the fundamentalist clerics in the Guardian Council, an institution that safeguards the interests of the conservative establishment.

In society, women activists increased their vibrancy; they held numerous workshops and training programmes with new subjects such as eliminating violence against women, women's share in power, and equal rights in divorce and inheritance, which used to be taboos before this period. The supports of the administration improved the position and rights of women in the upstream policy documents, including the Five-year Development Plans, though any formal and legal shift still had to be in the framework of the traditional Islamic discourse of the supreme leader.

The dominant discourse and policy of the regime, however, was re-tuned when the conservative establishment helped a radical, former-militant candidate, Ahmadinejad take the administration through the 2005 presidential elections. In parallel, fundamentalists and formerly military figures took the majority of seats in the parliament through engineered elections and sought to continue the manipulation of the laws concerned with women's rights (Ehteshami & Zweiri, 2009). Securitisation and co-optation of the critical women movements intensified since that election.

As for the formal discourse, the Ahmadinejad administration echoed the traditional rhetoric of the supreme leader about women and their position. 'Women should be the source of comfort at home, the comfort of men'; this sentence represents the core of Khamenei's discourse about women (2014). He has also always delegitimated feminism by labelling it as a Western school of thought that promotes the sexual exploitation of women. In line with this discourse, Ahmadinejad purged women with liberal or feminist profiles from the administration and replaced them with fundamentalists. Many of his state officials had an affiliation with the Islamic Revolutionary Guard Corps (IRGC), the ideological militia of the regime, and traditionalist Islamic seminaries under Khamenei's office. As for the centre for women's affairs in his office, the then president picked two women that openly talked about a U-turn from improving political participation of women towards strengthening motherhood (Mehrkhaneh, 2013). This change in the state isolated the voice of feminist leaders and changed the balance of power between the traditional women and feminist ones in civil society.

When the conservative discourse was translated into policies and praxis, the main goal of it was getting women back from work to home. For instance, the state cabinet passed a set of bills and enactments that reduced women's working hours and introduced gender segregation in workplaces (Mehrkhaneh, 2014). Moreover, public budgets were allocated to the women activists and groups that were the loyal forces for implementing programmes, workshops, schemes, and policies that were mostly concerned with Hijab, motherhood, marriage, and the commitment of women to children's upbringing. The titles of the national and local schemes reflected this conservative approach, for example, the scheme of Enabling Rural Girls – focused on teaching the skills for house making – and the Mercy project for training thousands of women about the functions and features of a Muslim Family. Some policies had a strong element of force in them, for instance, the so-called 'Moral Police' scheme that deployed police forces to the streets in major cities to check and control women's outfits and head-wearing in the public (Yeganeh, 2012). Many of the state policies were designed and implemented in cooperation with military forces and especially the IRGC (Sadeghi, 2009a, 2009b).

Conservative representatives in the parliament promoted a similar approach and restricted women's social presence and education rights by referencing Quranic texts, such as the one 'the heaven is under the mother's foot' which prioritises homemaking over social activism, an NGO president said in her interview. Parliament, for example, passed a bill on defining quotas for women in technical university courses, and the localisation law, that was meant to make female students be admitted to state universities in their hometowns (Dustdar, 2020).

In the society, dozens of local and national fundamentalist and conservative women NGOs were set up and received funds from the state institutions and military forces. At the same time, the outspoken and critical NGOs had to go through a verification and re-registration process where many of them were disqualified and shut down. By doing this, the government engineered and homogenised the composition of civil society in favour of Islamist women NGOs. Also, the state offices shut their doors on the remaining outspoken feminists and conservative, religious women were given an active insider position in commissions and committees. In parallel, the Ministry of Interior in the first term of the Ahmadinejad administration increased the number of security clearances required to be obtained from security and police forces for registering an NGO. As a result, many feminist women faced administrative and political hurdles in officially registering a group. As an NGO president mentioned in her interview, obtaining permission for public programmes such as demonstration or training workshops became harder or even impossible, despite the articles of the constitutional law about the freedom of assembly and organisation. Even in some cases, when women activists organised gatherings on the streets without official permission, they faced threats and repression by the police, for example in 2007 in Hafte-Tir Square of Tehran, 70 feminist figures were arrested during a demonstration (Kar, 2006).

In addition, the security forces resorted to Article 610 of the Islamic Penal Code, which is about punishments of conspiring to commit crimes against security, to push back critics and activists (Faghihi, 2020; Noghrekar, 2019). Consequently, dozens of female students and workers in associations, organisations, and syndicates, were charged with 'colluding against the regime' that either took them to prison or left them with no way but to levelling down their activities.

While in the 2005–2009 period, women still had some limited chances of criticising the state policies in media outlets, civic spheres, and social media; from 2009, the restrictions intensified. After the ninth presidential elections and the second victory of Ahmadinejad, the nationwide Green Movement, with the presence of millions of people in large cities protested what it called a 'fraudulent election.' In response, the establishment and administration hand in hand with the military forces initiated hard repressions and intensified the security system which also had consequences for the women's rights movements. Ahmadinejad openly called his rivals 'dirt and dust' in a public speech right after the elections, and following that, and a speech by Khamenei, the security and military forces levelled up pressures and suspicion over the critical NGOs and perceived them as 'spies and traitors' (Abdi, 2010). The then-president particularly took a more radical stance against NGOs, when he said 'since there are religious foundations, there is no need for NGOs' (Radio Zamaneh, 2011). Due to the increase in the costs of critical activism, many women activists had to give up their organised activism and flee Iran to avoid arrest and several others were taken to prison. The government also revoked the licence of opposition political parties, such as the Participation Front of Iran, which had a progressive women league. Dozens of newspapers and magazines, including women's publications like *Iran-Dokht*, were banned, and stopped publishing after a judicial order (Aftab, 2010). At the same time, many new state-funded social media pages, websites, and newspapers appeared that propagated the mandates of the leader and president concerning women.

Any contact and cooperation of NGOs and feminist activists with international organisations were forbidden, and this policy was more destructive for women NGOs and leaders, because it first paralysed them financially as they were no longer able to receive funds from abroad, and second, several female activists were arrested after they took part in international events in other countries. This made the second decade of the 21st century the period of over-securitisation for the leading figures of the feminist women movements. Nevertheless, these shifts did not mean that women movements died. To compensate for their exclusion from politics, feminist women had to resort to the few surviving media and online platforms, as well as the remaining active political parties. In a few cases, feminist NGOs had no choice but to make a coalition with conservative counterparts to save the basic rights of women that were at risk. For instance, in the second term of the Ahmadinejad administration, in the case of amending the Family Laws in favour by introducing the right of polygamy for men, a rainbow coalition of women activists from both reformist and conservative camps, mass media, and NGOs succeeded to stop the implementation of the law and made the parliament step back and revise it (Sadeghi, 2009a, 2009b).

In 2013, through the tenth presidential elections, the so-called moderate camp returned to power with the victory of Rouhani and ruled the country until 2021. But the measures for controlling feminist NGOs and women's rights activists remained in place. The Rouhani administration used a mixed discourse that included on the one hand the elements of eliminating gender violence to satisfy the educated modern women but at the same time the conservative's rhetoric of family empowerment with an emphasis on the role of women. During this period, several policy developments institutionalised the supervisory and controlling role of security and military forces over civil society organisations. In parallel, Khamenei and the Islamic organisations under him uplifted their stress on strengthening the family role of women and increasing the population. This was an obstacle for the feminist streams with the 'gender equality' approach; hence, again, the feminist leaders and activists remained behind the doors of government and parliament. In November 2020, the conservative parliament passed a law that required increasing childbearing by making contraception illegal. Few women's rights organisations protested it, but meanwhile, state-funded women groups with the privilege of receiving public finance were deployed to villages and small towns to encourage and train families to have more children.

Since 2020, this trend of the regime intensified when in addition to the government's pressures, two more changes took place. First, the global Covid-19 pandemic provided the regime with an excuse to increase militarisation by expanding the areas of activity especially for the IRGC and Basij forces. By pushing back and isolating the independent NGOs and volunteer groups across the country, the government deployed the military forces on streets and public spheres instead of providing volunteer forces with more space to act against the health and social crises, while in parallel the security forces increased pressures on the critical social and print media. This worsened the situation not only for the civil society groups but also for women, particularly in the areas of femicide and violence (Pirnia et al., 2020). In March 2021, the Global Gender Gap Report demonstrated the constant declining status of women in Iran. While in 2006, after a period of limited political reforms, Iran was ranked 108th globally, in 2021, it dropped in the ranking to 153 out of 156 studied countries (World Economic Forum, 2021). The Iranian women workers lost their jobs 14 times more than men due to the health crisis, meaning a sharp fall in their financial independence compared to the opposite sex (Tajdin, 2021). Before that, reports had been showing an increase in the number of honour-killings; more than one-quarter of the total number of murders that took place.

The second shift was the rise of Raeesi, a former judge who contributed to the execution of thousands of political prisoners in the 1980s, to power alongside his fundamentalist camp in the 2021 presidential elections. His administration narrowed the women's issues to the family issues and promoted the plans and policies in the area of growing the population, for example by reducing working hours for women and defining for them a significant role in the long-term policy of increasing the population size of the country. Raeesi's Minister of Interior expressed a statement that symbolises the ultra-pessimism of the government about the women movement; he said: 'if the Islamic Revolution is to be hit by someone, it would be done by women.'

Hence, female civil leaders had to step back to struggle for repealing their fundamental rights. This has limited demands and expectations, which are more about the basic rights of women, compared to the 1990s.

## Conclusion

In the last four decades, women's rights leaders and groups resorted to all the possible civil and electoral methods to reform the regime policies; but the formal ideology and policies at the top of the state remained unchanged. The regime resorted to securitisation, militarisation, and Islamisation constantly and gradually to nullify feminist streams. In the long-term, this made women activists more dispersed, contained, and suppressed. This policy was followed by a period of controlling the movement through legal manipulation during the Rouhani administration and restricting the women activists during the Raeesi administration. In 2020, the Covid-19 pandemic provided the regime with an excuse to militarise politics and civil society.

Currently, although the vibrancy and voice of women's movements sound to be higher in the 21st century thanks to social media, an increase in the number of female political prisoners shows the status of women in terms of freedom has been exacerbated. Nevertheless, the women movements have grown bigger in size to include different classes and strata of women. In recent years, the presence of women in the first lines of nationwide street protests and the increasing number of ordinary women alongside feminist leaders in prisons shows the growing impact of the women movement and the spread of feminist discourse in society. However, the constant radicalisation of the regime's policies and discourse concerning women's rights and organised activism have reversed the progressive trajectory of the women's rights movement in terms of their demands.

## References

Abbasi, S. (2014). A look at the position of iranian women in the Pahlavi era, from 1921 to 1953. *Journal of Women*, *1*, 59–82.

Abdi, A. (2010, April). 13 Millions of dirt and dust. https://p.dw.com/p/Mpgr. (D. Welle, Interviewer).

Abdolmohammadi, P., & Cama, G. (2015). Iran as a peculiar hybrid regime: Structure and dynamics of the Islamic republic. *British Journal of Middle Eastern Studies*, *42*(4), 558–578.

Aftab. (2010, March). *Closure of 20 reformist publications*. Retrieved from Aftab News Website: https://aftabnews.ir/fa/news/95736/.

Diamond, L. J. (2002). Thinking about hybrid regimes. *Journal of Democracy*, *13*(2), 21–35.

Dustdar, N. (2020, November). *University gender quotas: A story of frustration and discrimination*. Retrieved from Radio Zamaneh: https://www.radiozamaneh.com/550175/.

Ehteshami, A., & Zweiri, M. (2009). *Iran and the rise of its neoconservatives: The politics of Tehran's silent revolution*. I.B. Tauris.

Eisinger, P. (1973). The conditions of protest behavior in American cities. *American Political Science Review, 81*, 11–28.

Faghihi, M. (2020, February). *A legal quagmire that takes victims incessantly: Article 610 of the Islamic penal code*. Retrieved from Ensaf News Website: https://www.isna.ir/news/98050201052/.

Gheissari, A., & Nasr, V. (2006). *Democracy in Iran: History and the quest for liberty*. Oxford University Press.

Grant, W. (1989). *Pressure groups, politics and democracy in Britain*. Philip Allan.

Heydemann, S. (2010, October). Upgrading authoritarianism in the Arab world. *The Saban Centre for Middle East Policy, 13*. The Brookings Institution.

Kar, M. (2006, June 15). *Women and society: Women beaten in Hafte Tir square by security forces and women police; interview with Mehrangiz Kar*. Retrieved from Radio Farda: https://www.radiofarda.com/a/282568.html.

Karl, T. L. (1995). The hybrid regimes of central America. *Journal of Democracy, 6*(3), 72–86.

Khamenei, A. (2014, April). *Speeches*. Retrieved from Khamenei: https://farsi.khamenei.ir/photo-album?id=36210.

Kitschelt, H. (1985). New social movements in West Germany and the United States. *Political Power and Social Theory, 5*, 273–342.

Koopmans, R. (1999). Political. Opportunity. Structure. Some splitting to balance the lumping. *Sociological Forum, 14*(1), 93–105.

Lemarchand, R., & Legg, K. (1972). Political clientelism and development: A preliminary analysis. *Comparative Politics, 4*(2), 149–178.

Liverani, A. (2008). *Civil society in Algeria: The political functions of associational life*. Routledge.

Mehrkhaneh. (2013, July). Retrieved from Mehrkhaneh Website: http://mehrkhane.com/fa/news/7056/

Mehrkhaneh. (2014, June). Retrieved from Mehrkhaneh Website: http://mehrkhane.com/fa/news/7054.

Meyer, D. S., & Minkoff, D. C. (2004). Conceptualizing political opportunity. *Social Forces, 82*(4), 1457–1492.

Namazi, B. (2000). *Iranian NGOs: Situation analysis*. Hamyaran Center.

Noghrekar, M. (2019, July). A lawyer's proposal to remove article 610 of the penal code and amend the political crime law. (I. N. Agency, Interviewer) Retrieved from ISNA News Agency.

Pirnia, F., Pirnia, K., & Pirnia, B. (2020, October). Honour killings and violence against women in Iran during the COVID-19 pandemic. *The Lancet Healthy Longevity*.

Porta, D. D., & Diani, M. (1999). *Social movements: An introduction*. Blackwell Publishing Ltd.

Radio Zamaneh. (2011, July). *NGOs in the Islamic republic of Iran*. Retrieved from Radio Zamaneh Website: https://www.radiozamaneh.com/34010.

Sadeghi, F. (2009, Spring). Foot soldiers of the Islamic republic's "culture of modesty". *MER 250*. Middle East Research and Information Project.
Saeedzade, M. (1998). *What is the share of women in the civil society?* Ghatre.
Sedghi, H. (2007). *Women and politics in Iran: Veiling, unveiling, and reveiling.* Cambridge University Press.
Sadeghi, F. (2009). Foot soldiers of the Islamic republic's "culture of modesty". Middle East Research and Information Project, 39. Retrieved from http://www.merip.org/mer/mer250/foot-soldiers-islamicrepublic%E2%80%99s-%E2%80%9Cculture-modesty%E2%80%9D.
Tajdin, B. (2021, March 8). *Covid impact on women's employment in Iran; 14 times more than men.* Retrieved April 2021, from BBC Persian: https://www.bbc.com/persian/business-56323543.
Tarrow, S. (1989). *Democracy and disorder: Protest and politics in Italy, 1965–1975.* Clarendon.
Tazmini, G. (2013). *The Islamic republic and the turbulent path to reform.* I.B. Tauris.
The Centre For Women Participation. (2001). *The women's participation and the seventh government.* Iran's Centre For Women Participation.
Wigell, M. (2008). Mapping 'hybrid regimes': Regime types and concepts in comparative politics. *Democratisation, 15*(2), 230–250.
World Economic Forum. (2021, March 31). *Global gender gap report 2021.* World Economic Forum.
Yeganeh, B. (2012, February). *Ahmadinejad's support and the moral security police.* Retrieved from Radio Farda: https://www.radiofarda.com/a/f3_moralpolice/404570.html.

# 10 Effective Leadership
## Yemeni Local CSOs

*Elham Raweh*

### Introduction

This chapter sheds light on the Yemeni local CSOs working in peacebuilding activities and some humanitarian assistance, exploring their effective leadership in response to the local community's needs, in humanitarian assistance, in building peace, and in restoring social cohesion, throughout the CSOs' approaches in implementing projects, managing their staff, dealing with donors, and maintaining financial sustainability as the main factors of effective leadership in local CSOs. With more focus on the current phase challenges as the Covid-19 pandemic hit the world and its leaders could not do much to reduce its effects and stood almost with bare hands.

The tendency among scholars towards measuring the effective leadership of NGOs and CSOs is yet to have consensus (Forbes, 1998; Herman et al., 1996; Stone & Cutcher-Gershenfeld, 2001), as the concept of effective leadership or effectiveness performance is conceived in very different ways according to the evaluator (Herman et al., 1996; Yukl, 2013). CSOs have different forms and purposes (Herman et al., 1996). Some scholars relate the CSO's effectiveness to its board's effectiveness and one may lead to the other; however, this cannot be isolated from other main factors such as the executives and staff that might cause the effectiveness of the organisation and the board as well (Herman et al., 1996).

In research related to Yemen, there is a deficiency due to the deteriorated situation, which has resulted in Yemen being the forgotten war or known only for its humanitarian crisis (BBC News, 2015; Elayah & Schulpen, 2017; Kleemann, 2019). Left alone, the behaviour of local CSOs in Yemen during the conflict has been understudied. The majority of them work in humanitarian aid and relief which catches most of the attention; however, their performance, effectiveness, approaches, and methods are not highlighted enough.

The study uses a combination of heavy review for the available literature in descriptive methodology combined with personal interviews with head managers and executives of local CSOs working in peacebuilding activities and humanitarian assistance in order to investigate their way of doing and practising leadership.

## Local CSOs and Civil Society Actors

Civil society as a community sphere takes form through various types of associations (Barnes, 2005). These types are voluntarily formed, including non-governmental organisations (NGOs), community-based organisations (CBO), and civil society organisations (CSOs), such as youth and women-led organisations, groups, and initiatives, such as youth and women's groups and initiatives (Paffenholz, 2015). The civil society sphere gathers actors with different aspirations of diverse components and elements within any community (Barnes, 2005, p. 7). And within this space, they can build their skills and engage in the community and practice their leadership in many forms. It also promotes people-to-people dialogues and collaborations (Barnes, 2009).

The term 'civil society actors' includes local community-based organisations, associations, local CSOs, NGOs, youth, and women. The terms NGOs and CSOs are used interchangeably in this study according to the definition of CSOs concept in the document 'Partnership Framework between the Government of Yemen (GoY) and the CSOs' and the field assessment study 'Yemen CSOs in Transition' as:

> Civil Society Organizations CSOs are these non-governmental organizations NGOs, associations, or unions established by citizens, pursuant to the constitution, the laws and legislation in force, with the purpose of contributing to the public good, by providing services or funding in economic and social development, or conduct research, or advocacy, or public education. Expressing the concerns and values of a segment of community members on the basis of ethical, cultural, political, scientific, and religious or charity considerations without seeking to make a profit or achieve political power.
> (MoPIC and UNDP, 2013, p. 3; World Bank, 2013, pp. 13, 45)

## Yemeni Local CSOs and Effective Leadership

In Yemen, the civil society has evolved over the years forming different shapes and for different purposes. Yemen over time has witnessed countless forms of collective humanitarian and charitable work that is rooted in the heritage and culture of the society for a very long time (MoPIC and UNDP, 2013; Al-Mawri, 2019), which forms a practice of local leadership to respond to needs. The conditions of this civil cooperation and local leadership have been embodied in many works, such as building dams, cisterns, mosques, and roads, and also reached providing aid to low-income families, and solving local disputes (Al-Mawri, 2019). Civil society in Yemen is known to be vibrant and diverse, yet very fragmented with various civic groups along with less organised charity-oriented and local self-help groups (World Bank, 2013). Historically documented, the Yemeni civic engagement has its earliest by the 1950s, according to Sheila Carapico (1998) in her book *Civil Society in Yemen: The Political Economy of Activism in Modern Arabia*. Carapico outlines three periods of civil revival, which sets Yemen as an example of significant civilian progress in the region (Carapico, 1998; World Bank, 2013). In the first period from 1950 to 1963, there were around 45 civil society organizations (CSOs) founded in opposition to the British colonial rule in the south and the Imamate in the north (Carapico, 1998; World Bank, 2013; Qassim et al., 2020). The second is from the 1970s to late 1980s, with the growth in the number of CSOs to 424 organisations officially registered in 1989. The third phase, after the Yemeni union in 1990, along with its constitution of 1991 and the amended law in 2001. The law guarantees 'the state's commitment to parliamentary democracy, political pluralism, and a multi-party system' (Yemen Constitution, 2001). As a result of that, a 'transformation of traditional civil society (Mujtama al-Ahli) to more modern forms of civil society (al-mujtama al-Madani) accelerated' in this phase (Qassim et al., 2020).

There are several types of civil society institutions in the Yemeni law: associations, foundations, and unions. The Associations and Institutions Law (Law No. 1 of 2001) provides the legality to organise and form within associations, national organisations, cultural centres, CSOs, NGOs, and unions or clubs. A modified definition for association and foundation is found in Article 2:

> Any popular group established in accordance with this law by natural persons, the least number of which is 21 persons at the time of application for the establishment thereof, and 41 persons at the constituent meeting (members) for the association. Foundation can be established by one or more persons, and its membership is limited to the founder(s). The primary purpose for both is the realization of a common benefit for a specific social group, or to undertake activities or functions that are of a public benefit, and which does not seek from its activities to generate a financial profit for its members, and the membership of which shall be

open in accordance with the conditions spelled out in the organizational procedures.

(MoPIC and UNDP, 2013; World Bank, 2013; ICNL, 2020b)

Under this law definition, foundations, local CSOs, unions, or associations can be established by one or more natural and legal persons for the purpose of public benefit. All different types of associations, foundations (CSOs), networks, alliances, and unions must register with the Ministry of Social Affairs and Labor MoSAL in the capital of Yemen Sana'a or at the local MoSAL representative offices in the governorates (MoPIC and UNDP, 2013; World Bank, 2013; ICNL, 2020b).

The 1994 document of 'Pledge and Accord' was produced to solve the conflict between the North and the South. Along with different political and social factions at that time, CSOs and NGOs took part in reaching this 'historical document' as described by Elayah in an article of the national dialogues that took place in Yemen as an interruption of the civil war (Elayah & Verkoren, 2019a).

With reference to Carapico and the World Bank's outline mentioned above, a fourth and fifth period can be added to the growth of CSOs in Yemen. The fourth is from 2011 to 2015. By the end of 2011, more than 8,000 CSOs were registered with MoSAL (MoPIC and UNDP, 2013; World Bank, 2013). Sequentially, the transitional phase after 2011 has accelerated the civil society engagement with the community and the government with approximately 12,000 to 15,000 CSOs that took action in several areas either with or without being registered in MoSAL (Qassim et al., 2020). The newly founded organisations are led mainly by youth and women (Al-Mawri, 2019). Consistent with what Beshara (2017) highlights, most CSOs' leadership is usually from the upper and lower-middle class. In Yemen, they are also from the educated middle to a lower class with the majority of youth and women (AL/Intv17, personal communication, 2021; Beshara, 2017).

To some practitioners 'CSOs had an unprecedented opportunity to play a vital leadership role as an active partner with the government in a comprehensive development, especially with the donors' conference in Riyadh and the massive support by the donors' (MoPIC and UNDP, 2013; Al-Mawri, 2019). In September 2012, under the Government of National Reconciliation, the Mutual Accountability Framework was approved at the Riyadh conference in September 2012, emphasising the importance of engaging civil actors in Yemen's development and acknowledging the complementary leadership role of CSOs in promoting transparency, inclusive decision-making, and accountable policies (World Bank, 2013). As a result of that, with the support of the World Bank and in cooperation with CSOs, UNDP and the GoY led efforts to develop a partnership framework with the CSOs in September 2013 in order to serve the broad development goals in Yemen; this forms a new role for CSOs to play (World Bank, 2014).

Simultaneously, the Yemeni National Dialogue Conference (NDC) took place between March 2013 and January 2014. Within the Gulf Countries' Corporation (GCC) initiative and its implementation mechanism, it includes 565 representatives, not only from political parties but also from civil society actors such as local CSOs, NGOs, youth and women groups, and marginalised groups. It is inclusive for all political and social components and the first actual practice of total inclusivity that enables all society segments to sit at one table and discuss their persistent issues and lead the change as a practical example of the local leadership (Elayah et al., 2020; Fraihat, 2016; Papagianni, 2014; Zyck, 2014). NDC and its representatives were making it the first of its kind in Yemen – regardless of Yemen's past experiences in dialogue – and of its kind in the entire Arab world (Fraihat, 2016). NDC is considered to be a remarkable step towards a successful political transition; notwithstanding that, it failed to prevent the country from descending into a fierce war at that time.

Even though the partnership agreement and its framework have institutionalised the path for better cooperation between the GoY and the CSOs, 'in a step of its kind with a lot of efforts made to great progress achievement, elevated Local CSOs and local NGOs leadership' a Yemeni academic and expert explained, 'yet, it felled apart with the transitional process, and no major improvement has been made ever since' (AA/Intv4, personal communication, 2021).

From that on, the fifth phase of growth for CSOs in Yemen from 2015 until the present day can be identified. After, and as a result of, the conflict escalation in 2015, civic activism and its effective leadership has faced significant challenges and has consequently decreased (Colburn, 2021). Several CSOs had to pause or reduce their activities, or in a worse case, shut down. A poll's result that a research centre in Yemen carried out concluded that in 2015 almost '70% of Yemeni NGOs have been closed since the start of the armed conflict, while 60% of these organizations have faced several acts of violence, looting, provocation, harassment, or freezing of assets' (Elayah & Verkoren, 2019b).

Aside from that, there were several steps taken in order to monitor CSOs' activities and projects, and to a certain extent, restrict international and local NGOs by the existing government institution that is currently in charge of registering, reviewing, and evaluating the work of CSOs and NGOs. All organisations, either local or international, are required to do pre-coordination and seek permission to implement any activity beforehand (ICNL,

2020a). All types of activities (i.e., 'peace-related' activities or projects) are cut-off or delayed. As a result, it has hindered many international and local organisations and restricted the space for civic activism and effective leadership in general (Qassim et al., 2020).

This also lines up with Barnes's (2005) view, that it is hard for CSOs to thrive amidst lawlessness and widespread violence, and the space for civic activism and local leadership will be more limited (Barnes, 2005; Paffenholz, 2010). It became so difficult for local CSOs to participate in the political arena that oftentimes they shifted their work to humanitarian assistance instead (Qassim et al., 2020). However, one may say that several local CSOs have thrived throughout this period and adapted to the situation, which is quite similar to what happened during the transitional process in 2012 when CSOs remained undaunted despite the crisis (Caton, 2013). Moreover, it enabled them to be more robust towards responding to their local community's needs in the current crisis phase (Colburn, 2021). 'The situation urged the organizations to act quickly,' a local organisation working in Taiz assures. Local CSOs are closer to the local communities, knowing their dire needs and how to meet them best (AL/Intv5, personal communication, 2021; AL/Intv12, personal communication, 2021; AO/Intv22, personal communication, 2021).

That is, on the community level, there are the local actors who accompany the CSOs trying their best to be the first responders leading many initiatives that respond to the daily challenges faced by the people due to the perpetuated conflict consequences (AL/Intv3, personal communication, 2021; AL/Intv5, personal communication, 2021; AL/Intv6, personal communication, 2021). On the one hand, responding to the community needs, attempting to mitigate conflict effects, and on the other, maintaining their presence.

When it comes to internal challenges, several CSOs are facing financial crises and flight of skilled staff outboards due to the conflict (AL/Intv13, personal communication, 2021). Added to that, in a few local CSOs is the bad leadership or 'single leader' and weak skills to communicate or lead the organisation, 'unfortunately, transparency and good governance are absent in most organizational work in Yemen, and the individual and family nature is still dominant in most organizational work, and most of them lack strategic plans and visions for their work' answered a women-led organisation (AL/Intv6, personal communication, 2021). In other cases, a number of CSOs might affiliate with political parties or take one side of the conflict which affects many things in their implementation quality and ethicality, 'you might find some organizations that was founded by one political party or another in order for them to maintain the civil work as well' said an executive manager (AL/Intv9, personal communication, 2021). This has its affects in two ways; one on the organisation favour and the other on politicians, where they would pass through the organisation work their agenda and use the assistance delivery to get their support from a wide range of people and beneficiaries. The local CSO's favour would be in getting more funds and expediting their implementation. However, in both cases, the local communities are the ones who get harmed (AL/Intv9, personal communication, 2021).

Refering back to leadership effectiveness, the tendency among scholars towards measuring the effective leadership of NGOs and CSOs is yet to have consensus (Herman et al., 1996; Forbes, 1998; Stone & Cutcher-Gershenfeld, 2001), as the concept of effective leadership or effectiveness performance is conceived in very different ways according to the evaluator (Herman et al., 1996; Yukl, 2013). CSOs have different forms and purposes, 'capable and reliable partners depends not only on the skills of the managers, employees and service volunteers in those organizations but also on the commitment and skills of their boards of directors' (Herman et al., 1996). Some scholars relate the CSO's effectiveness to its board's ability and effectiveness and one may lead to the other; however, this cannot be isolated from other main factors such as the executives and the rest of the staff that might cause the effectiveness of the organisation and the board as well (Herman et al., 1996). To reflect this on the Yemeni local CSOs and NGOs, during the interviews, it was shown that this is not the case in all of them. Some have a board of trustees and others only have the head of the organisation who controls everything financially and administratively, and in better cases, CSOs have the board of trustees as names on paper with no actual presence (AL/Intv4, personal communication, 2021). This kind of one-leader or what is known as 'centralised leadership' is a main challenge in numerous CSOs not only in Yemen but also in other communities such as the Congo Basin (Almeras, 2018). Other scholars might stress the organization's leader ability to 'optimize the human resources' and their ability to lead the organisation staff to its success and their leadership style (Lwin, 2019), and in Yemen, 'many organizations still facing the lack of equality leaders and leadership skills in general' said an executive manager of a local CSO in Aden (AL/Intv11, personal communication, 2021).

## Leadership Aspects (Strategic Plans and Financial Sustainability)

Going back to how possible it is to measure the effectiveness of the Yemeni local CSOs, one might choose a strategic plan as one clear indicator of the effectiveness and the 'development of alternatives or modifications to the goal model of effectiveness' (Herman & Renz, 2004). It is common sense that should CSOs have strategic plans and goals; however, when asking the interviewees of the local CSOs about their strategies and plans, some assured of the intention to update their existing plans once more funding is received and some others found it difficult to do so in the current situation with various challenges such as security, donor's applications, limited resources and funds; a head of an organisation added: 'we had to adapt and change our areas of work to line with the situation and the donors' demands' (AL/Intv6, personal communication, 2021). The CSOs in the current time are facing multiple challenges and obstacles, administratively, financially, and with respect to security, said a CSO working in Taiz governorate (AL/Intv10, personal communication, 2021), because of the lack of training and capacity-strengthening programmes due to the deteriorated situation inside the country, flight of the skilled cadre, with low wages compared to the rising prices of commodities and life expenses.

On another aspect of effective leadership, financial sustainability is considered as a measurement that can indicate whether a CSO is in a good condition to maintain and preserve its work and mission, or is just living on the availability of funds applications. 'We don't have income sources, the only resource we have is the fund that we apply for and receive from the donors. We keep searching for any fundraising opportunities in order to maintain our presence' said a local CSO working in Abyan (AL/Intv9, personal communication, 2021), noting the cut-off fund to peace-related, long-run programmes and activities and shift to emergency response or Covid-19 response. This has a huge implication for the CSOs working in specific programmes towards building peace, development, or social cohesion activities. In addition to that, and as a result of Covid-19 implications, there were a number of humanitarian agencies that reduced their work 'due to lack of funding,' which hindered the local CSOs' ability and leadership and would aggravate the humanitarian situation in the country as a whole (ReliefWeb, 2021).

## Conclusion

In many situations, local CSOs are the closest to the local communities and able to respond to their need with more audacity in time and size. They also play an important role in the country's development and improvement. However, the increasing number of local CSOs in the community can be alert to the low effectiveness of these organisations and their unsustainability. Measuring their effectiveness is impossible with the lack of data and records of these organisations.

## References

Al-Mawri, A. (2019). Institutional capacity building as an entry point to strengthen the partnership between the government and civil society organizations in the Republic of Yemen, 51.

Almeras, E. (2018). The challenge of leadership in civil society organisations in the Congo Basin. Well Grounded. https://well-grounded.org/wp-content/uploads/2018/04/Leadership-Discussion-Paper-Eng_FINAL.pdf.

Barnes, C. (2005). Weaving the web: Civil society roles in working with conflict and building peace. In P. van Tongeren & European Centre for Conflict Prevention (Eds.), *People building peace II: Successful stories of civil society* (pp. 7–23). L. Rienner Publishers (A project of the European Centre for Conflict Prevention).

Barnes, C. (2009). Civil society and peacebuilding: Mapping functions in working for peace. *The International Spectator*, *44*(1), 131–147. https://doi.org/10.1080/03932720802693036.

BBC News. (2015). Inside Yemen's forgotten war. *BBC News*, 11 September. Accessed December 3, 2020. https://www.bbc.com/news/world-middle-east-34211979.

Beshara, A. (2017). *Civil society: A critical study*. Arab Center for Research & Policy Studies.

Carapico, S. (1998). *Civil society in Yemen: The political economy of activism in modern Arabia*. Cambridge University Press (Cambridge Middle East Studies). https://doi.org/10.1017/CBO9780511584893.

Caton, S. C. (2013). *Yemen*. ABC-CLIO.

Colburn, M. (2021). *A new path forward: Empowering a leadership role for Yemeni civil society*. Yemen Peace Forum: Sana'a Center For Strategic Studies, p. 44. Accessed April 11, 2021. https://sanaacenter.org/publications/main-publications/13021.

Elayah, M., & Schulpen, L. (2017). *Yemen: A forgotten war and an unforgettable country*. https://doi.org/10.13140/RG.2.2.33827.04649.

Elayah, M., Schulpen, L., van Kempen, L., Almaweri, A., AbuOsba, B., & Alzandani, B. (2020). National dialogues as an interruption of civil war – The case of Yemen. *Peacebuilding*, *8*(1), 98–117. https://doi.org/10.1080/21647259.2018.1517964.

Elayah, M., & Verkoren, W. (2019a) Civil society during war: The case of Yemen. *Peacebuilding*, *8*(4), 476–498. https://doi.org/10.1080/21647259.2019.1686797.

Elayah, M., & Verkoren, W. (2019b) Civil society during war: The case of Yemen. *Peacebuilding*, 1–23. https://doi.org/10.1080/21647259.2019.1686797.

Forbes, D. P. (1998). Measuring the unmeasurable: Empirical studies of nonprofit organization effectiveness from 1977 to 1997. *Nonprofit and Voluntary Sector Quarterly*, *27*(2), 183–202. https://doi.org/10.1177/0899764098272005.

Fraihat, I. (2016). *Unfinished revolutions: Yemen, Libya, and Tunisia after the Arab spring*. Yale University Press.

Herman, R. D., & Renz, D. O. (2004). Doing things right: Effectiveness in local nonprofit organizations, a panel study. *Public Administration Review*, *64*(6), 694–704. https://doi.org/10.1111/j.1540-6210.2004.00416.x.

Herman, R. D., Renz, D. O., & Heimovics, R. D. (1996). Board practices and board effectiveness in local nonprofit organizations. *Nonprofit Management and Leadership, 7*(4), 373–385. https://doi.org/10.1002/nml.4130070404.
ICNL. (2020a) Civic freedom monitor – Yemen. *International Center for Not-profit Law*, 3 April. Accessed December 4, 2020. https://www.icnl.org/resources/civic-freedom-monitor/yemen.
ICNL. (2020b) *Yemen, international center for not-for-profit law*. Accessed March 26, 2021. https://www.icnl.org/resources/civic-freedom-monitor/yemen.
Interview No.3, anonymous. (2021). [Via Zoom].
Interview No.4, anonymous. (2021). [Via Zoom].
Interview No.5, anonymous. (2021). [Via Zoom].
Interview No.6, anonymous. (2021). [Via Zoom].
Interview No.7, anonymous. (2021). [Via Zoom].
Interview No.8, anonymous. (2021). [Via Zoom].
Interview No.9, anonymous. (2021). [Via Zoom].
Interview No.11, anonymous. (2021). [Via Zoom].
Interview No.12, anonymous. (2021). [Via Zoom].
Interview No.17, anonymous. (2021). [Via Zoom].
Kleemann, S. (2019). The forgotten war: Yemen. Universitätsverlag Potsdam. Online veröffentlicht auf dem Publikationsserver der Universität Potsdam https://doi.org/10.25932/publishup-43071
Lwin, N. N. (2019). Impact of leadership style on employee engagement in civil society organizations in mandalay region. Yangon University of Economics, Management Studies.
MoPIC and UNDP. (2013). Partnership framework between the government of Yemen and civil society organization | UNDP in Yemen. Accessed December 4, 2020. https://www.ye.undp.org/content/yemen/en/home/library/democratic_governance/partnership-framework-between-the-government-of-yemen-and-civil-.html.
Paffenholz, T. (2010). *Civil society & peacebuilding: A critical assessment.* Lynne Rienner Publishers.
Paffenholz, T. (2015). Civil society and peacebuilding. *Development Dialogue, 63*, 108–118.
Papagianni, K. (2014). National dialogue processes in political transitions | HD Centre. European Peacebuilding Liaison Office (EPLO). Accessed March 29, 2021. https://www.hdcentre.org/publications/national-dialogue-processes-in-political-transitions/.
Qassim, A., Amin, L., Transfeld, M., & Strzelecka, E. (2020). *The role of civil society in peacebuilding in Yemen – CARPO e.V.* BRIEF 18. GIZ, BMZ, CARPO, p. 17. Accessed December 4, 2020. https://carpo-bonn.org/en/18-the-role-of-civil-society-in-peacebuilding-in-yemen/.
ReliefWeb. (2021). A letter from civil society organizations to the humanitarian coordinator in Yemen. Tamdeen Youth Foundation. Accessed October 9, 2021. https://reliefweb.int/report/yemen/letter-civil-society-organizations-humanitarian-coordinator-yemen-enar.

Stone, M. M. & Cutcher-Gershenfeld, S. (2001). Challenges of measuring performance in nonprofit organizations. In P. Flynn & V. A. Hodgkinson (Eds.), *Measuring the impact of the nonprofit sector* (pp. 33–57). Springer US (Nonprofit and Civil Society Studies). https://doi.org/10.1007/978-1-4615-0533-4_3.

World Bank. (2013). *Yemen civil society organizations in transition: A mapping and capacity assessment of development-oriented civil society organizations in five governorates*. World Bank Other Operational Studies 16638. The World Bank. Accessed December 4, 2020. https://econpapers.repec.org/paper/wbkwboper/16638.htm.

World Bank. (2014). *A new role for civil society in Yemen, World Bank*. Accessed April 10, 2021. https://www.worldbank.org/en/news/feature/2014/03/04/a-new-role-for-civil-society-in-yemen.

Yemen Constitution. (2001). Yemen's constitution of 1991 with amendments through 2001. Accessed December 4, 2020. https://constituteproject.org/search?lang=en&q=Yemen&status=in_force&status=is_draft.

Yukl, G. (2013). *eBook PDF for leadership in organizations: Global edition*. Pearson Education.

Zyck, S. A. (2014). *Mediating transition in Yemen: Achievements and lessons*. International Peace Institute, p. 20.

# 11 Conclusion
## Impact and Ways Forward

*Ibrahim Natil*

This book significantly contributes to theoretical discussions of the power of CSOs' leaders who have challenged the complexities imposed by Covid-19 and the serious shifts made to CSOs' scope of work owing to health conditions and circumstances. It has presented a new approach to arguments and discussions about the concepts and practices of CSOs' leadership in the field of development and engagement by analysing various cases from different cultures and locations. It has provided the reader with a firm theoretical framework of CSOs' leadership and development issues that are relevant not only for an academic audience but also for international agencies, policymakers, and practitioners active in Brazil, India, Yemen, Syria, Iran, Turkey, and Palestine. By assessing contexts and engaging policymakers with rigorous empirical research in a systematic way, CSOs' leaders' engagement can work to overcome both the internal and external challenges they face.

The leadership of third sector comprises non-governmental and not-for-profit organisations, volunteers, charities, and CSOs undertaking a diverse mix of support and representation activities with a dedication to a particular societal issue or group. Many of these are brought together voluntarily to work towards collective interests and have long histories of challenging political adversaries, such as with CSOs. The third sectors in Western countries, however, are part of active democracies that also engage a range of social and political groups in governments' decision-making processes. However, the pandemic is causing a human development crisis affecting social groups and marginalised communities worldwide. The third sector therefore has the opportunity during this time to exercise a real leadership to push governments towards collective interests and responsibilities. For example, there have been leaders whose use of digital tools to conduct peacebuilding dialogue can amplify pre-existing marginalisation of certain groups, which hampers genuine and inclusive participation and risks elite capture adding new layers to conflicts. Furthermore, the absence of international organisations on the ground due to travel restrictions is causing accountability and bias issues amongst CSO leaders.

The book thus enriches the current debate on CSOs' leaders' skills, knowledge, and power to balance the demands and needs of their internal organisations (technical, financial, and human resources) on one side and their local communities' needs on the other. This pushes CSOs' leaders to balance community needs and their organisational sustainability to deliver in the fields of civic engagement, development, and local peacebuilding. This shows the power of young CSOs' leadership, their influence on grassroots engagements, their capacity to strengthen local networks, and their undertaking of effective actions in times of crisis and landscape shifts. CSOs' leaders have succeeded in employing alternatives to technology to improve the engagement of marginalised groups who have no access to the internet, which diminishes the control of certain classes over civic space, dialogue, and community peacebuilding initiatives.

This book will assist undergraduates, postgraduates, scholars, and professionals in understanding CSOs' leaders' experiences in adapting and engaging while challenging shifts and changes within their societies. It covers mostly intermediate and advanced levels for Master's students and full-time academics in the educational sphere, but it will also be useful for professionals working in development and business. The book will also be of interest to the general public and will contribute to the fields of development, peacebuilding, conflict resolution, civil society, and foreign aid and to the study of politics, business, management, and international relations. This will assist students in these subjects as the book is widely researched and is very relevant to courses on development studies, international development, and business, as well as advanced courses on the international political economy and courses on the politics, government, and civil society of the Middle East, Asia, and Latin America. It distinguishes itself as a new approach to civil society in the global context by focusing on leadership and development.

It has studied the impact of political, social, and economic dynamics and structures that influence the leadership of CSOs at the local, national, and global levels. It has focused on challenges facing CSOs' leaders' societal contributions, current operational practices, and strategies for future development. It has also focused on new leadership lessons from the field of CSOs, and the chapters have examined experiences and cases studies of CSOs' leaders' performances, challenges, and engagement in civil society activities. It has discussed leadership and civic engagement challenges and the impact of digital technology and social media in responding to shifts due to Covid-19 while young CSO leaders have been challenged by foreign aid and financial shifts. These issues are vitally important to understand these changes to the perspectives of community development, civic engagement, local peacebuilding. However, technical challenges and educational initiatives have been delivered by CSOs' leadership structures.

From my personal experiences in the non-profit sector at all levels, I have met many CSO leaders from different locations, cultures, and backgrounds around the world who succeeded in founding CSOs with various scopes of work, missions, visions, and goals. These leaders, for example, motivated volunteers with various professional backgrounds to serve as board directors or trustees when establishing the CSO's legal framework, which is a condition to serve and function as a legal body, which assists CSOs with being accountable before their general assemblies, local authorities, and local and/or foreign donors. The overwhelming majority of these CSO leaders, however, remain in their positions, functioning as chief executive officers (CEOs) for a long period, which could be considered a negative issue for CSOs in the long term despite the structural and/or leadership sustainability. This model of leaders could build a solid network at the local and international level, serving CSOs' programmes, fundraising efforts, vision, and mission.

In other words, long-term positions reflect the image of CSOs and the personalisation of the business. There have been a number of CSOs that have linked their images with the fame of their CEOs, which promotes stereotyping and the misperception of CSOs within their own societies to some extent. It creates a public impression that the CSO is controlled by its leader or CEO, who is charismatic and powerful after a long period in the position. The younger generation is not given chances to exercise their leadership skills and visions at a high level, which promotes rotation within the CSOs' hierarchies. The absence of younger leadership will cause strategic problems once the long-term leader steps down for any reason. I observed that a number of CSOs that were led for a long time by charismatic Palestinian and Jordanian leaders who left their civil society space for public or civil servant positions as a diplomat or a politician suffered at the operational and leadership levels and caused their ultimate closure. This example of leadership failed to prepare a future leadership structure or to assist in moving the CSO forward by encouraging the pool of volunteers and the board of directors to lead effectively. There are models of volunteers who engage or serve as board directors/members for personal goals, networking, benefits, or other incentives, such as seeking an opportunity to travel abroad, training, etc. In other words, they are not motivated by the CSOs' charismatic leadership. Their motivation to contribute to the process of change for their societies is not always a top priority.

Young people, however, are more much motivated to join CSOs to acquire experiences, skills, and knowledge by participating in various training opportunities and contributing to organising community events and civil society spaces. Young people or students are motivated by CSOs' charismatic leaders who inspire them with the values, activities, and future opportunities of civil society. This type of civic engagement or voluntary participation assists young people to build their CVs while undertaking undergraduate or postgraduate studies or while looking for a job. In other words, the indirect or direct influence of charismatic leaders on young people is greater than for well-established or professional people.

The book, thus, brings a heightened awareness of the challenges involved but also highlights the potential for greater policy engagement for CSOs' leaders to change policies, e.g., to eradicate poverty. The main contribution of the book has been to undertake new research, particularly around informed practice on the ground, and present recommendations to policymakers and donors on better ways of providing space for young people and their CSO contributions on specific policy issues. We hope this book has provided insights and that it will stimulate others to conduct research in this growing area. In particular, it has listed some implications and offered some directions for future research in the fields of leadership, business, and development in non-western societies.

It has also introduced the lessons learnt by CSOs' leadership structures in responding to technical constraints and improper policies, despite the existence of social conservatism, conflict, violence, and the absence of democracy and exclusive political systems in a number of countries. Moreover, the situation on the ground makes it difficult for their staff to work normally. Yet, they are trying hard to achieve and respond to the community's needs, and in order to maintain and improve this role, there are some recommendations that can be adapted to better effectiveness of local CSOs' leadership. CSOs' leaders, however, may work on strengthening capacity of their local staff and volunteers with more designed programmes and specified for organisations, which works on humanitarian assistance, peacebuilding activities, development, and long-term programmes.

CSOs' leaders should consider building a strategic partnership with government bodies and international organisations by re-implementing the strategic partnership plan and designing new partnerships that lead to better programmes and localisation of development and humanitarian assistance. They, however, should focus on developing an equal partnership with donors and long-term collaborations. This partnership should consider allocating more funds for institutional improvement for those local CSOs and NGOs. This requires the CSOs' leaders to have strategic plans and risk mitigation plans by donors and international funders and partners. More importantly, leaders should engage with their local partners and grassroots to share budget information, expenditures, and the process of implementation.

## Conclusion 125

This will increase transparency of funds spending and better equality in implementing humanitarian and development programmes and projects.

These issues and considerations are significant to secure and acquire new mechanisms for the sustainability of funds and self-generating budgets. The Covid-19 pandemic, however, has profoundly shaken the ways CSOs' leaders support and engage with researchers and practitioners working in/with CSOs in the Global South and the Global North. The banning of public gathering and human face-to-face interaction, travel restrictions, and shrinking of funding are only some of the critical challenges that CSOs' leaders have been facing over the last years.

CSOs' leaders attempt to show the advantages of different groups working together for their mutual benefit and tangible results to engage victims in participating in social and political activities. The participatory process is also associated with the practice of a top-down mechanism conducted to include citizens' engagement and contribution to the public sector. The central argument in the investigation of this main issue is contrary to wide assumptions that CSOs and their leaders in unstable circumstances and divided societies have no room or power to influence society and become engaged in the development of their society or support active participation while enduring uncertainty and shifts such as the Covid-19 pandemic. Future research may explore, share, and reflect upon the challenges that have affected CSOs' work and research and how practitioners and researchers have dealt with them.

# Index

authoritarianism 5, 55–61, 64, 98, 101

civic space 1, 122
civil society 1–14, 16–25, 28–38, 41–52, 55–64, 68–78, 80–95, 98–107, 110–117, 121–122
civil society organisations (CSOs) 1–14, 16–25, 28–38, 41–52, 55–64, 68–78, 80–95, 98–107, 110–117, 121–125
community-based organisations 2, 111
Covid-19 1, 3–5, 8, 11, 12, 28, 29, 37, 42, 43, 45, 48, 63, 94, 107, 118, 121, 125
CSOs *see* civil society organisations
cultures 1, 3, 5–7, 12, 22, 121

development 1–4, 7–12, 18, 25, 41, 42, 44, 46, 72, 73, 80, 81, 87, 117, 118, 121
dialogue 4, 5, 28, 31, 35, 36, 38, 111, 114, 121

engagement 1–14, 16–25, 28–38, 41–52, 55–64, 68–78, 80–95, 98–107, 110–117, 121–125
equality 1–14, 16–25, 28–38, 41–52, 55–64, 68–78, 80–95, 98–107, 110–117, 121–125

financial uncertainty 1
Freedom of speech 77

Global South 2, 125

human rights 2–4, 7, 10, 12, 56, 60, 61, 63, 64, 76

INGOs *see* international non-governmental organisations
innovative 1, 2, 8, 17, 19, 20, 24, 83
international donors 2, 3
international non-governmental organisations (INGOs) 2, 28, 29, 31, 37
intervention 1, 10, 30

justice 1–14, 16–25, 28–38, 41–52, 55–64, 68–78, 80–95, 98–107, 110–117, 121–122

leaders 1–14, 16–25, 28–38, 41–52, 55–64, 68–78, 80–95, 98–107, 110–117, 121–125
leadership 1–5, 10, 12–14, 16–25, 28–38, 41–52, 55–64, 68–78, 80–95, 98–107, 110–117, 121–125

management 1–25, 32, 81, 84, 89, 90, 122

NGOs *see* non-governmental organisation
non-governmental organisation (NGOs) 1–14, 16–25, 28–38, 41–52, 55–64, 68–78, 80–95, 98–107, 110–117, 121–125
non-profit organisations 1, 2, 10, 12, 13, 82, 121

operations 1, 3, 17, 18, 22, 23
organisations 1, 2, 8, 12, 18, 20, 23, 38, 51, 52, 56, 57, 80–82, 84, 87–89, 91, 101, 104–106, 111–113, 115, 122

pandemic 1, 2, 4, 8, 28–30, 32, 37, 43, 45–47, 94, 107, 125
peacebuilding 3–5, 7, 12, 14, 28, 29, 31–38, 110, 111, 121
Platform 4, 12, 28, 62, 88

rights-based approaches 2

scholars 1, 3, 24, 116
social restrictions 1
strategies 1, 2, 9, 14, 83

third sector 6, 10, 80–82, 84, 88, 91, 93, 121

volunteers 2, 12, 17–19, 47, 49, 52, 86, 116, 121, 123, 124

women's rights 2, 5, 6, 10, 11, 56, 98–109

youth 4, 41–44, 51, 52

For Product Safety Concerns and Information please contact our EU
representative GPSR@taylorandfrancis.com
Taylor & Francis Verlag GmbH, Kaufingerstraße 24, 80331 München, Germany

www.ingramcontent.com/pod-product-compliance
Lightning Source LLC
Chambersburg PA
CBHW051752230426
43670CB00012B/2251